Presented to:

LINES

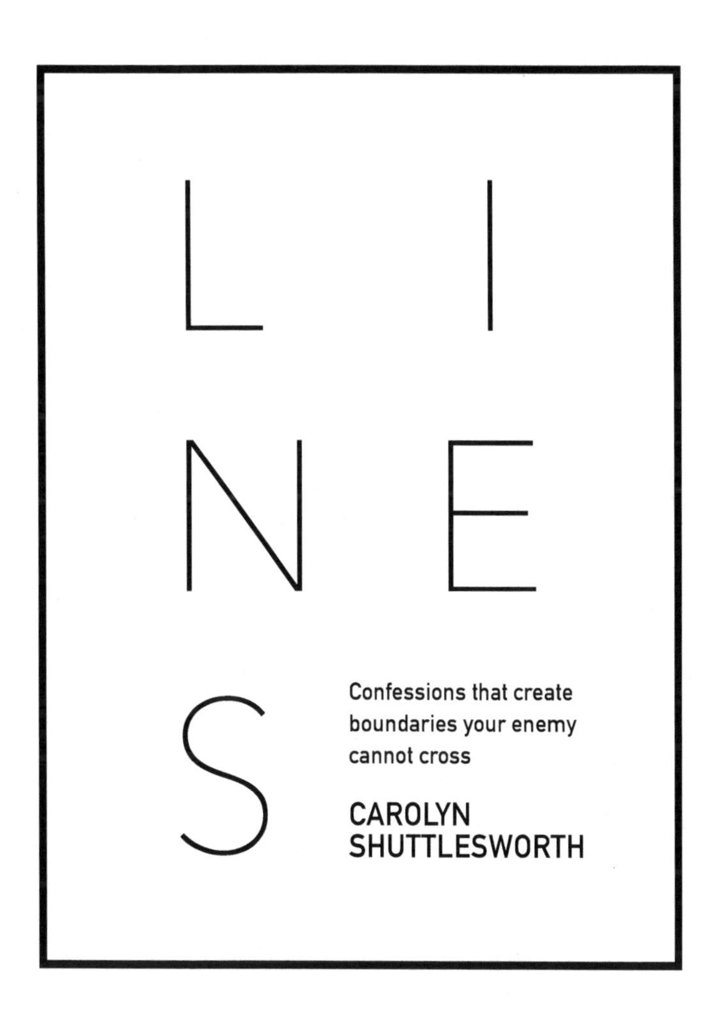
LINES
Confessions that create boundaries your enemy cannot cross
CAROLYN SHUTTLESWORTH

MIRACLE WORD
PUBLISHING

Published in Virginia Beach, Virginia by Miracle Word Publishing.

Miracle Word titles may be purchased in bulk for educational, business, fund-raising, or sales promotional use. For information, please e-mail info@miracleword.com

All uppercase and italicized text in verses of scripture are added by the author for the purpose of emphasis.

ISBN 978-1-7349962-1-0

Printed in the United States of America

For my husband, who continually challenges me to grow, and for my children who are learning to stand their ground at a young age.

INTRODUCTION

> *"My heart rejoices in the Lord! The Lord has made me strong. Now I have an answer for my enemies; I rejoice because you rescued me."*
>
> *1 Samuel 2:1 NLT*

There comes a time when we say, "Enough is enough." We have a benefits package that comes with our salvation covenant. Jesus told his disciples that he had given them authority over all the power of the enemy (Luke 10:19). Authority is released through the power of our confession.

Faith comes when you hear the Word of God (Romans 10:17). You become spiritually strong as your faith is continually built.

Your confessions come from what you *already* believe about God's Word. The apostles said, "We believe therefore we speak." It's vitally important that we have proper beliefs about God and his Word. If we don't, our confessions won't carry the divine power that brings change.

That's why I not only provide a declaration and a prayer each day of this devotional, but I also provide Scripture. Everything must be based upon God's Word.

Don't allow natural circumstances or someone else's experience to govern what you say or do in God's kingdom. His Word is the only standard that should define your life.

My prayer is that as you read this book and release these powerful confessions, you will be filled with a fresh boldness and rise to new levels of faith.

Let's create boundaries around your family, health, finances, and mind that the enemy cannot cross. He has trespassed long enough. It's time to live in full freedom and victory in Jesus' name. Let's get started!

DAY 1

CONFESSION

"I am the body of Christ. My body is the house of God. Nothing can remain that isn't from him."

Don't you realize that your body is the temple of the Holy Spirit, who lives in you and was given to you by God? You do not belong to yourself,

1 Corinthians 6:19 NLT

It's a very interesting concept to be part of the body of Christ. The Bible says that God made Jesus to be the head over all things to the church, which is his body (Ephesians 1:22-23).

If we're a part of his body, then we are literally a part of him. We are Christ. We're not different beings; we are in him.

When you introduce yourself to someone, you don't say, "Nice to meet you. My head is Ashley, and my body is Carol." Your head and body are one and the same.

We need to understand our relationship with Christ in

the same way. When the devil tries to attack your body with sickness, he's attacking Christ's body with sickness. He doesn't have the authority to do that. What cannot harass Christ cannot harass you.

The next time the devil tries to infringe on your covenant, stand on this revelation, and command him to go. He cannot touch Christ's body.

PRAYER FOR TODAY

Thank you, Lord, that I'm part of Christ's body. His Spirit and power live in me. The devil has no authority to harass me because Jesus defeated him. I walk in wholeness. I live in divine healing, and I rebuke the enemy who comes against my covenant.

DISCUSSION QUESTIONS

1. What are some things that come to mind that you know cannot harass Christ? (And thus cannot harass you!)

2. What does being in the body of Christ afford you?

3. Is any kind of sickness ever in God's plan or will for you?

4. What does "living in wholeness" mean?

5. How will you treat and care for your body knowing you are the body of Christ?

DAY 2

CONFESSION

"Jesus has given me the gift of peace of mind and heart. It is a gift the world cannot give or take away."

You will keep in perfect peace all who trust in you, all whose thoughts are fixed on you.

Isaiah 26:3 NLT

This is one of my go-to verses. We have to realize how essential this verse is to our well being. It sets a standard of living for us.

This verse shows us two things about how to live in perfect peace. First, you must trust in the Lord with all of your heart (Proverbs 3:5-6), and second, be in control of your thoughts. We must take the Word of God at face value.

Remember the story of Peter walking on water? I've read that story my whole life, but as I've gained wisdom and revelation of the Word, when I read those verses, I now envision a concrete sidewalk stretching out to Peter when Jesus calls him.

When Peter *trusted* the literal word of the Lord and fixed his *thoughts* on him, Peter was able to start walking on the water towards Jesus. It wasn't until he started paying attention to the storm and its effects around him that he began to sink.

We shouldn't pay attention to the things around us that could cause fear, doubt, and unbelief. Be in charge of your atmosphere. Keep your home, yourself, and your family in perfect peace.

PRAYER FOR TODAY

Thank you, Jesus, for this wonderful gift of peace. It is a vital part of my life. I will make sure to receive this gift you have given to me and operate in its fullness. I command peace be still in my finances, in my marriage, with my children, with my decisions, in my mind, and in every area of my life.

DISCUSSION QUESTIONS

1. Is a peaceful heart and mind your current standard of living right now?

2. What does a peaceful thought life look like to you?

3. What opens the door to fear, doubt, and unbelief?

4. What does taking the Word of God at "face value" mean?

5. What are some practical ways to take charge of your atmosphere?

DAY 3

CONFESSION

"Jesus is my hiding place and will protect me from trouble."

Fear not, for I am with you; be not dismayed, for I and your God; I will strengthen you, I will help you, I will uphold you with my righteous right hand.

Isaiah 41:10 ESV

I'm sure we will never forget the outbreak of COVID-19 in 2020. Never in our lifetime has virtually everything shut down, and fear gone completely rampant. With everything that was being said, I was often asked how it did not affect me.

Here is a perfect example where reading and studying the Word comes into play. Anyone who follows me on social media knows that is the one thing I stress the most.

I was raised in church and thought I knew the Word until I really started studying it for myself and making time to pray and gain revelation and wisdom.

The beginning of the verse above starts with "fear not." That alone is enough instruction for us. When we are obedient, we receive the blessings of God (Joshua 1:8). So if "fear not" was our only instruction in Isaiah, that would be enough, but it goes on to tell us *why* we should fear not.

As children of God, we have an incredible benefits package that comes along with our covenant. Just like you have natural benefits that may come with your job, you receive a benefits package when you're saved, as well.

We always make sure we get what we paid for. The same goes for our heavenly benefits package. Make sure you are getting everything that was promised to you. It pays to understand what belongs to you.

The Lord told us not to feel distressed or alarmed. He will give us strength, help, and will hold us above anything that could harm us. God's mighty right hand is far more powerful than anything a man could offer us.

PRAYER FOR TODAY

Jesus, I will make sure to go after your Word and gain an understanding of what you have for me. You are my protection at all times. I will use my benefits package to live at my full potential—how a child of God should live.

DISCUSSION QUESTIONS

1. Can you remember a specific time you know the Lord protected you from trouble? If you're in a group, share your testimony with others! If you're alone, take time to remember and thank him.

2. Did you experience the truth of God's Word in your home and family during the 2020 outbreak of COVID-19?

3. How do you guard yourself from thoughts that are filled with fear?

4. How do you currently (or how will you now begin) to ensure your knowledge of the Word of God only ever increases?

5. What are some of the benefits given to us in our covenant with God? What's in your "benefits package?"

DAY 4

CONFESSION

"Jesus promised me rest for my soul, not struggles."

Then Jesus said, "Come to me, all of you who are weary and carry heavy burdens, and I will give you rest."

Matthew 11:28 NLT

We should not be going from crisis to crisis and struggle to struggle. At some point, our faith needs to demolish what's hindering us so we can live a life of freedom and blessing. If this is something you're battling, don't think there is no hope. You can absolutely walk in that kind of faith. We have to realize that as long as we are on this earth, there will be no cap on our faith level.

There are Christians unnecessarily walking around in a struggle. I don't want to keep hearing how people's most important lessons come from the trials in their life. Let me clear up a few things. First, although he prophesied persecution, Jesus did promise an easy life. Throughout the Bible, we are told if we walk in obedience, we'll experience God's overwhelming blessings.

Second is the verse I mentioned above. We will find rest for our souls because his burden is light. We don't have to go through struggles to better understand our heavenly Father.

This message isn't always an easy one to swallow because it puts the responsibility on us. The Bible tells us in Hosea 4:6 that we can perish for *our* lack of knowledge. We don't have to go through crises the way society does and then pay the big bucks to be counseled out of them.

When I started Nonstop Mom, I happened to be reading 1 Samuel 2:1 and came across Hannah's prayer. I stand on it daily. That is how I want to operate as a woman of God! She was full of praise, joy, strength, and knowledge. None of that sounds like a person who is struggling. I know it's possible, and I'm standing in agreement with you as you read this.

PRAYER FOR TODAY

I pray that my wisdom and revelation of the Word will increase, and I will be fully stocked with ammunition to fight off any attacks of the enemy. Today, I will be free and rested by the power of Jesus' name!

DISCUSSION QUESTIONS

1. What does a "struggle-free" day mean to you personally?

2. If we perish because of our lack of knowledge, what is your game plan to make sure that doesn't happen?

3. Can you think of anything in your life that you have the power to change to feel more rest and less struggle?

4. What does the next level of faith look like to you?

5. What will you do to get to that next level of faith?

DAY 5

CONFESSION

"I will never perish because I have knowledge of the Word. I will always be a student."

My people are destroyed for lack of knowledge; because you have rejected knowledge, I reject you from being a priest to me. And since you have forgotten the law of your God, I will also forget your children.

Hosea 4:6 ESV

You don't ever want to be on the sidelines, not knowing what's going on. Every day, we have an opportunity to gain knowledge. When we read Hosea 4:6, we have to understand what it means to perish. Perish defined means to "suffer death typically, in a violent, sudden, or untimely way." That's pretty intense, but it doesn't have to be that way. It's time we get back to the Word and fill ourselves up.

I know many of you are very busy. We are career women, wives, mothers, or caretakers. We know how to fill our time with many details. At the end of the day, did we fill it with the right things?

There is always something we can give up to spend more time building our spirit man. We have to live in battle-ready mode. I understand we have already won the victory, but I see too many Christians who think they're prepared, then they receive a bad report or hear a lie from the enemy and become weak.

Never allow yourself to get to the place where you become unteachable. The student will never be greater than the master (Jesus Christ), *but* we have to strive toward that goal. He gave us specific instructions about how we were to live after he left the earth.

If we never learn what they are or how to bypass the enemy's tricks, we will grow cold spiritually—and that bleeds over into the natural realm.

PRAYER FOR TODAY

Lord, anoint my mind to gain wisdom and revelation of your Word. I am focused, and I am teachable. I will make time to learn what you have set aside for my life and use that to do great things for your Kingdom.

DISCUSSION QUESTIONS

1. Have you filled your life with anything that's crowding in on your personal time with God and the study of his Word?

2. Do you have a strong spirit man? Why or why not?

3. What were the specific instructions Jesus gave us when He left the earth about how we are to live?

4. How do you intentionally make time to study the Word of God every day?

5. If a battle began tomorrow, are you prepared with the right ammunition?

DAY 6

CONFESSION

"I will live by every word that proceeds from the mouth of God."

But if you stayed joined to me and my words remain in you, you may ask any request you like, and it will be granted!

John 15:7 NLT

It's so vitally important that we grab ahold of this confession and verse. By what words are you living? Are you living by what your co-workers say about you? Are you living by what your past says about you? Are you living by what society says about you? This can destroy your thinking, causing your thoughts to spiral out of control. It will change the way we live, and we could even end up changing our beliefs to wrong doctrine, ideas, and confessions. Your confession has to line up with the Word of God to receive what it says you can have.

The Bible says we are the head and not the tail (Deut 28:13). He meets all of our needs (Matt 6:33). He takes away worry and anxiety (1 Peter 5:7). He gives us peace (John 14:27). He wants us to live in divine healing (Acts 10:38). The list of his goodness is long and has been spoken over our lives. We have to take what God said at face value. If we don't know what our heavenly Father has said about us or the situation we are in, we will believe any words we hear.

If my daughters never heard "I love you" from their father or me, they would believe the first guy who said it, and that person could lead them down the wrong path. But because we fill our girls with strong words of affirmation, they are grounded in what they know and can't be persuaded otherwise.

God made a masterpiece and didn't make any mistakes (Eph 2:10). The correct words over your life are the fuel to your spirit man. If the enemy ever tries to tell you otherwise, you already have a leg up.

PRAYER FOR TODAY

Thank you, Lord, for making me. I will find out what has been spoken over me by reading the Bible. I will take your words at face value and live by them daily. Knowing what my authority will take me to new levels of faith in Jesus' name!

DISCUSSION QUESTIONS

1. Have you let anyone's words take root in your life that contradict what God says about you? If so, what does the truth of God's Word say about those areas?

2. What does it mean to live by "every word that proceeds from the mouth of God?"

3. Remind yourself of some of the things over which Christ has given you authority.

4. Is your faith gaining new strength every day? How?

DAY 7

CONFESSION

"I have the wisdom to lead and teach my children."

But if any of you lacks wisdom, let him ask of God, who gives to all generously and without reproach, and it will be given to him.

James 1:5 NASB

This is something I find myself declaring a lot. I am a mom of three, and I homeschool two of them for the time being. Once my youngest is old enough, he will be thrown in the mix, too. Some days can feel like a heavier load than others, but I find great joy in knowing the Lord has chosen me to be the teacher—not just with school but as a parent.

The Bible says in Proverbs 22:6, "Teach your children to choose the right path, and when they are older, they will remain upon it."

Sometimes we can feel unqualified or wonder if we're doing things correctly. The wonderful thing is God has entrusted and anointed you to do this very task. Just like the verse above, all we have to do is ask God for help.

If we get to a point where we feel like we aren't making an impact or we don't know what to do in a situation raising our children, the Lord will answer our prayer and give us the words to say, how to say them, and how to show them.

Having three kids means different personalities and learning styles, so I've had to do things in three different ways. Even so, the Lord knows exactly how to show me the way.

It might not always be the easiest, but the great thing is he has anointed us for even the hard times. When the Word of God tells us we can do all things through Christ, that applies to *every* situation in life.

Ask the Lord today to help you in your parenting life, whether it be more patience, kindness, love, or even how to discipline. The Lord will show and teach us so we can do our jobs properly. He'll never rebuke us for asking. He's waiting for us to ask. Let's do our part so God can perform his part.

PRAYER FOR TODAY

Thank you, Lord, for my children. They are a blessing in my life. Use me to raise them in a godly way. Anoint my mind so I can be the best teacher in their life. Please give me the correct words to keep them on the path you have chosen for their life. Use me to build them up to be a mighty man or woman of God!

DISCUSSION QUESTIONS

1. What is something specific the Lord has been teaching you as a mom?

2. List some of the ways your children are a great blessing to you.

3. How is the Holy Spirit involved in your parenting right now?

4. What is something you're believing God to do for your children this month?

5. Think of at least one specific action you can do today to build up and encourage each of your children.

DAY 8

CONFESSION

"I am a woman of strength. I am a woman with a sound mind. I am a woman with stable emotions. I am a woman with an answer for her enemies."

For we are God's masterpiece. He has created us anew in Christ Jesus, so that we can do the good things he planned for us long ago.

Ephesians 2:10 NLT

This confession needs to be ingrained in our minds and spoken daily. As women, it can be easy to let our emotions go bananas and wear them on our sleeves. I've been at fault for this, but as I have grown in understanding of what the Lord says about me, it has become less and less frequent over the years.

You weren't created to be weak, a basket case, constantly stressed, stupid, or ugly. A masterpiece is a work of outstanding skill or workmanship. Jesus did not make a "hot mess." When I see shirts that say, "Jesus loves this hot mess," they make me cringe. It may not seem like a big deal, but women start to live by that saying. It will justify their actions. "I can be any old way, and Jesus will still love me." Correct. Jesus will still love you, but will others? Will others still want to be around you?

Society has made us believe we are supposed to be this overly emotional being. Yes, Jesus did make us different than men based on our roles, but we can't use that as an excuse to become women without self-control. We are women of worth, and we need to start declaring it over our lives and thinking that about ourselves.

PRAYER FOR TODAY

Thank you, Jesus, for making me a perfectly crafted woman. You knew what you were making. I am royalty and an heir to the throne of God. I will start acting like it. My thoughts and actions will be an example of the fruit of the Spirit when I come into contact with others.

DISCUSSION QUESTIONS

1. What are some ways you can carry yourself as royalty and as a masterpiece made by God?

2. Are you honestly keeping your emotions under control on a consistent basis, or do they rule your life? How will you ensure you are emotionally stable?

3. Are there things in your life that needlessly cause you stress? If so, how can you make a change?

4. What are some practical things you can do everyday to build a peaceful atmosphere?

5. A peaceful life doesn't mean life isn't happening or that everyone is silent. What does a peaceful home mean to you?

DAY 9

CONFESSION

"Jesus took all sickness and pain, which now gives me the right to reject it."

But he was pierced for our rebellion, crushed for our sins. He was beaten so we could be whole. He was whipped so we could be healed.

Isaiah 53:5 NLT

When Christ died on the cross, we have to realize that he redeemed us from the curse of sickness and disease. Once he did that for us, he handed us the authority to reject it. We have to leave on the cross what belongs on the cross. The only thing that came down from the cross was Christ so he could fulfill his purpose on earth.

Leave sickness and disease on the cross. Don't think for one minute that God uses sickness to teach us a lesson. I don't teach my children about third-degree burns by wrapping their little fingers around my hot curling iron. I simply tell them what it does if they were to touch it.

It's the same for the Word of God. It tells us how to live in divine healing. It shows us how to have great faith and to live in the benefits package of our covenant. The words in the Bible are alive and powerful, and reading them and taking hold of them benefits us greatly.

The life of the Word gives life to our mortal bodies. As my husband says in his book *Blood On The Door: The Protective Power of Covenant,* your life shouldn't look the same as somebody who doesn't have a redeemer.

Our bodies aren't created to carry burdens; they are created to carry the blessings of God. Today, walk in your divine healing. If you don't feel like you're quite there in your faith, don't retreat. Press in harder and study healing in the Word.

The Bible shows us in Proverbs 37:25 that children of God don't have to beg for our healing because it already belongs to us.

Imagine a party where there is a gift table. All the presents have your name on the tag. Would you stand in the opposite corner staring at that table saying, "Look at those beautiful gifts. Oh, how I wish they were mine. Give me, give me, give me!" No! Jesus already gave you all those gifts. You simply must take them. When something is given to you, you become the owner. When we own something, we don't have to assume it's ours. *It is!*

PRAYER FOR TODAY

Every organ, muscle, and nerve in my body functions perfectly the way God created it to function. Every disease and every virus that touches my body dies instantly. Your Word is a part of me. It keeps me alive and well all the days of my life, in Jesus' name. Amen!

DISCUSSION QUESTIONS

1. What are some of the things that stayed on the cross?

2. What should the life of a redeemed person look like?

3. How does your body carry the blessings of God today?

4. Is sickness ever sent to you by God? How do you know?

5. What are some of the gifts Jesus has made available to us because of the cross?

DAY 10

CONFESSION

"I declare your Word over my mind.
I declare your Word into my spirit.
My life matters greatly."

The Lord is close to the brokenhearted; he rescues those whose spirits are crushed. The righteous person faces many troubles, but the Lord comes to the rescue each time.

Psalm 34:18-19 NLT

It angers me to hear of this spirit of depression and suicide that's running rampant. It's a murderous spirit that needs to be destroyed. Jesus hasn't made a mistake in creating anyone. Everybody is somebody to Jesus. We need to figure out what the Word says about us so we can take authority over the devil's lies. If we don't know how great God made us, what plan he has for our life, or how much power we hold over the enemy, we can easily fall prey to destruction.

Suicide or self-harm only seems like an option when

the devil has hidden all other options. We have to get into the Word of God so our eyes can be open to the truth.

Job 10:12 says, "You gave me life and showed me your unfailing love. My life was preserved by your care." To preserve means to maintain in its original or existing state. We have to remember that anyone alive with breath in their body has hope. Say, "I am alive. Jesus, you are my eternal hope."

This may not be a declaration for you, but for someone you know. If it's for you, I encourage you to get these verses in your mind and heart. Study your identity in Christ. If this isn't for you, make sure you encourage people with the truth of God's Word.

We may think people have it all together. They have happiness and joy, but behind closed doors, they are losing it. Robin Williams was a perfect example. He was paid millions of dollars to make people laugh. From the outside, it looked like everything was great, but he news of his suicide was devastating.

Let's not wait until we find out about these tragedies. Be someone who compliments, shows love, tells people about Jesus, and shows others how to walk in authority.

PRAYER FOR TODAY

Thank you, Jesus, for making me a perfect creation. You give me life and hope. I will do great things because you are my heavenly Father. I rebuke the lies of the enemy. He has no say over my life. Show me the path you have for me, and I will do great things for your kingdom.

DISCUSSION QUESTIONS

1. Who are you in Christ?

2. Can you pinpoint any area of your identity that is based on a lie (contradicting the Word of God)? Ask the Holy Spirit to open your eyes and show you.

3. Are you someone who builds others up at every opportunity?

4. What hope do we find in Jesus?

5. Did this topic make you think of anyone? Take time to pray specifically for them today and reach out with the encouragement and life found in the Word of God.

DAY 11

CONFESSION

"God makes me an expert in my field of work. The mind of Christ already sets me first in line."

Do you see a man skillful in his work? He will stand before kings; he will not stand before obscure men.

Proverbs 22:29 ESV

The Bible talks about God giving us the desires of our hearts. Those desires are placed there by God so we can implement his ideas on the earth. We are filled with the Spirit of the living God to bring divine ideas into existence. If we are Spirit filled, then we have no excuse not to have favor in the workplace or when learning new things that are beneficial to our lives. The Bible says in 1 Corinthians 2:16, "For who has known the mind and purposes of the Lord, so as to instruct him? But we have the mind of Christ [to be guided by his thoughts and purposes]." Our minds need to reflect the mind of our heavenly Father.

Nothing I've done in life was the result of an educational degree. Before I had kids and took off full time on the road with my husband, I worked in a law office. I started as a receptionist, but as I watched the attorneys and paralegals work, I became interested in what they did for real estate closings. I didn't go to school for any of that; I simply applied my mind of Christ to learning.

One of the real estate paralegals became pregnant and had to take leave. All of a sudden, I found myself in her position. I went from sitting in the receptionist chair to sitting in the conference room, handling real estate closings as people signed all their major closing documents.

I was then promoted to become the other real estate paralegal in the office, and worked with agents and major banks. With my promotion, I received bonuses and a financial increase in my pay. I had no prior training or schooling for what I was doing. With the help of the Lord, he positioned me for increase and future tasks.

Never feel like your promotion is out of your reach, even if you're a stay-at-home mom. You can have God-given ideas come to pass and make millions while sitting on your couch in pajamas. Let God use you and yield to the ideas and instructions he gives. He wants to see his children prosper.

PRAYER FOR TODAY

Jesus, thank you for empowering me with the Spirit of God, skill, intelligence, knowledge, and with all kinds of creativity to accomplish great works. I have the mind of Christ! No more excuses from me.

DISCUSSION QUESTIONS

1. What desires has God given you?

2. How are you stewarding the gifts God has given you?

3. Can you think of any specific excuses to excellence you have given recently? If so, how can you now fix that?

4. What would promotion look like to you?

5. How are you setting your faith for that promotion in action?

DAY 12

CONFESSION

"I am a tither and a giver. I am blessed financially."

Should people cheat God? Yet you have cheated me! "But you ask, 'What do you mean? When did we ever cheat you?'" You have cheated me of the tithes and offerings due to me!

Malachi 3:8 NLT

This step of our Christianity is vitally important. It means everything to us, to the utmost extreme. If you notice my declaration above, I wrote tither *and* giver. Those are two separate things. When I was little, I always heard this verse, but never understood the significance of doing *both*. I look at it much differently today. Now I see this verse through wisdom and revelation. Both tithing and giving produce something different. Let's start with tithing.

The Bible says in Deuteronomy 14:22, "Put on one side a tenth of all the increase of your seed, produced year by year." Our tithe is not "giving," and we have to understand the importance of the tithe. It's just handing back to the Lord what is already his. We are returning it to him in the same way you'd return your neighbor's borrowed laptop. When you go to bring it back, you don't say, "Look what I bought you!" No, It's already theirs. You're simply returning it to the owner. It's completely separate from your offering. The tithe keeps us under the blessings of God.

Now the offering. The Bible shows us in Luke 6:38 that our seeds (offerings) will be multiplied back to us by God. Our offerings bring increase into our lives. He gives us extra, overflow, and more than enough so that not only are our needs met, but we can provide for others.

While we are living on this earth, God wants us to be financially blessed. We don't have to wait until we're in Heaven to receive the finer things of life. Tap into all that God has for you on earth. If we're barely getting by, how can we fulfill the instructions to provide for others?

PRAYER FOR TODAY

Jesus, you are my supplier, and I never have to worry about lack. I'm obedient to your Word, and you grant me abundant prosperity. You push me to the front of the line. Because of my overflow, I am always looking for someone to bless. This will cause joy in my life and to the recipient.

DISCUSSION QUESTIONS

1. What would financial overflow look like for you and your family?

2. Can you remember a time (or many times) when God met a very specific financial need in your life? If you're in a group, share your testimony with others. If you're alone, take time to praise and thank him.

3. Have you been setting your focus on "lack" or the "supplier"?

4. How will you ensure that your giving this year exceeds the last?

5. Who is someone you can financially bless this month? How is the Holy Spirit directing you to do it?

DAY 13

CONFESSION

"I will remain teachable at all times."

But the Helper (Comforter, Advocate, Intercessor–Counselor, Strengthener, Standby), the Holy Spirit, whom the Father will send in My name [in My place, to represent Me and act on My behalf], He will teach you all things. And He will help you remember everything that I have told you.

John 14:26 AMP

Sometimes we get thrown into the unknown. We may accept roles for which we feel unqualified. You must always remember that you're anointed to do things you never saw yourself doing. Jesus has given us the mind of Christ, but we have to get out of our comfort zone. Christians are to be led by God's Spirit. When he gives an instruction, we must be ready to obey immediately.

When it came time for my firstborn to start school, I decided to homeschool. I never planned on doing this when

I had kids. I never gave it a thought. I never felt like I wanted to, but because of our ministry travel schedule, I decided to look into it. I had to fight off a lot of thoughts of not being good enough and not giving my children a "proper" school life. What is that anyway?

As a side note, don't be led to believe your children won't have social skills or will miss out on things because they are homeschooled. Could it be that weird homeschoolers are produced by odd parents? (Just an observation...)

I have been doing homeschool for over five years now, and I love it. I never thought I could do it as well as I have, but God has given me the grace to carry out what was new to me.

As Spirit-filled Christians, we have no excuse to be ineffective. As you can see in the verse above, the Holy Spirit wears many hats. That's good news for us. We don't have to search for help. He is a one-stop-shop.

I once heard my friend, Pastor Joie Miller (who has a powerful women's ministry in Pittsburgh) say, "We are anointed to do hard things!" That is absolutely right! When God reveals his secrets, we have access to his thoughts and ways that are higher than our own (Isaiah 55:8-9).

Tap into that ability that he has given you. Tap into the unknown, and let the Holy Spirit take the lead. Stay teachable, and God will use you to do things you never saw yourself doing.

PRAYER FOR TODAY

Lord, you have anointed my mind to do things I never saw myself doing. Thank you for opening up other avenues of increase in my life. I am fully capable of handling every new idea you give me and every new field that comes my way. I will continually build my knowledge and give you glory along the way!

DISCUSSION QUESTIONS

1. Have you ever felt unqualified to do what God has called you to do? What does the truth of God's Word say?

2. What is an area of your life you were hesitant to try or continue in because it simply looked too hard? How did God help you?

3. Is the Holy Spirit pinpointing an idea or a calling on which you have delayed taking action? If so, what will you do about it?

4. How will you remain teachable at all times?

5. Does letting the Holy Spirit be your teacher remove the requirement of diligence on your end?

DAY 14

CONFESSION

"Fear has no right to enter my mind. I refuse to allow the lies."

For God has not given us a spirit of fear and timidity, but of power, love and self-discipline.

2 Timothy 1:7 NLT

First, we need to know where lies originate. The Bible tells us in John 8:44, "For you are the children of your father the devil, and you love to do the evil things he does. He was a murderer from the beginning and has always hated the truth. There is no truth in him. When he lies, it is consistent with his character; for he is a liar and the father of lies." Now that we understand where all lies come from, we need to be strong enough not to believe them.

Jesus died so we can be totally free. Fear is an invisible prison that locks us in bondage. In 2 Corinthians 10:5, we are instructed to take *every* thought captive and make it obey Christ. He has given us authority that can't be stripped from us unless we surrender it to the enemy.

The choice is always ours. That is why it's so important to get true wisdom and revelation from the Word of God, so we don't fall prey to the enemy. There are times we hear something that causes instant fear. It's not anything we have personally experienced; it's just a "suggestion" of what could happen. Don't let the lies of the enemy corner you and have you make decisions on the "could happen" lie.

Know what the Word says about every situation, whether it be prosperity, peace, freedom, healing, love, etc. Defeat every attack with the power of your confession. Faith comes by hearing and hearing the Word of God. Make sure your ears hear faith-filled confessions coming out of your mouth.

PRAYER FOR TODAY

Keeping my mind on Jesus will root me in perfect peace. I will not give in to the lies of the enemy. I am suited and armed with the Word of God, and can deflect any lie that comes my way. I know who I am in Christ and understand the weapons with which he has equipped me. Today, I'm free from any invisible prison in which the enemy may try to lock me!

DISCUSSION QUESTIONS

1. List some ways that we hand our authority over to the enemy.

2. How do you take every thought captive?

3. Have you surrendered any area of your life to an invisible prison? If so, what action will you take today?

4. What are some fears you have conquered and been set free from in the past?

5. What does a fear-free mind mean to you?

DAY 15

CONFESSION

"I submit to my husband as to the Lord. I respect and honor him as the head of our home."

And further, submit to one another out of reverence for Christ.

Ephesians 5:21 NLT

Would you like to have a wonderful marriage the way God planned? God wants you to have unity in your marriage, and he has given us a biblical picture of how a Christian marriage should look. I know the word *submit* is one we are programmed by society to hate, but it's God's system of authority.

God's eternal Word provides specific instructions regarding proper order so that your home and relationship will run smoothly.

If you read past verse 21, the husband is commanded to love his wife the way Christ loves the church. That's the husband's submission to God's Word. When our husbands love us in that way, our role of submission is very easy. However, whether it's easy or not, we're still required to be submissive.

You can't go wrong by showing honor in any situation. Unless your husband is asking you to disobey the Word of God, it is your duty to follow his lead. We should speak highly of our husbands. We shouldn't discuss his flaws with our friends.

I know many of you reading this may be thinking, *there's a lot that my husband needs to change,* but remember, our job is not to nag him but to pray for him and praise him. Let the Holy Spirit work on the rest.

The Bible tells us in Colossians 3:13 that we are to make allowances for the faults of others. We aren't supposed to rub them in each other's faces and bring up all the things we don't like about a person. Wives are called to be a fountain of blessing to their husbands. If you stay in your biblical role, whether times are easy or frustrating, the Holy Spirit will help you with the rest.

PRAYER FOR TODAY

Thank you, Lord, for making me a strong wife. I will pray for my husband. I will honor my husband. I will love my husband unconditionally. I will have self-control over the words that come out of my mouth. I will have self-control of my thoughts. Thank you, Jesus, for showing me how to honor and submit to my husband the way your Word teaches.

DISCUSSION QUESTIONS

1. How are you a "fountain of blessing" to your husband?

2. What does a wonderful marriage mean to you?

3. Are there currently any areas of dishonor or disrespect in your heart towards your husband? If so, what does the Word of God say?

4. What does submitting to your husband as the Bible teaches bring to your marriage?

5. What are some specific ways you will pray for your husband today and this week?

DAY 16

CONFESSION

"I will meditate on God's Word. My knowledge of his Word will constantly increase."

God blesses those who hunger and thirst for righteousness, for they will be satisfied.

Matthew 5:6 NLT

Sometimes I feel like we can set ourselves up for failure in the area of personal devotion. We set a goal in our minds about when we'll have devotional time and how much we want to read. We can become really dedicated for a while, and then, suddenly, something in our schedule begins to steal our time.

The previously available time slot is now filled with kids' sports games, a new workout routine, or a new baby. We could find things to fill every hour of the day. Sometimes it's a lack of prioritizing our time, but I realize that sometimes we can't help it.

For example, moms are needed around the clock. We

sleep in small doses, can't go to the bathroom alone, and fix snacks every five minutes. (Can I get an amen?) I've learned that in each season, we have to find time to study the Bible.

When I had my first baby, I used to think being in church was enough—and I was in church a lot. That wasn't the case. I needed to do more, and I wanted to do more. The Bible says in Jeremiah 15:16, "When I discovered your words, I devoured them. They are my joy and hearts delight, for I bear your name, O Lord of Heaven's Armies." When you truly discover and "eat the Word," you become hungry for more and more!

Don't stress yourself out with how much you are doing in life at that moment. Your available time will be different in every season. Instead, focus on what you're meditating on. If you are a mom to a new little one, get some verses printed, and as you go about your day with the baby, receive wisdom and revelation from that one passage before moving on.

Eventually, in another season, you'll be able to spend more time in the Word. Never stop ingesting the Word. As the Bible says, the ones that hunger and thirst for righteousness will be filled. The ones who continually ingest the Word remain in supernatural joy. That creates a peaceful atmosphere.

PRAYER FOR TODAY

Jesus, I thank you that you honor your Word. As I gain an understanding of your Word, you will fill me with wisdom and revelation. In every season, I will pursue all that God has for me.

DISCUSSION QUESTIONS

1. What does your personal Bible study time look like right now? Are you satisfied with this, or does a change need to happen? What will you change?

2. What are some creative ways to keep the truth of God's Word in your heart and mind?

3. What is an area or topic in which you desire a stronger biblical foundation? Make a plan for when and how you will dig the truth and revelation out of God's Word for yourself.

4. What verse(s) have you personally been standing on this month?

5. Are your days too busy? What can you adjust to make sure your time with the Lord—whatever that may look like for you right now—is prioritized and not set aside?

DAY 17

CONFESSION

"I will not let my compassion hinder my faith."

His descendants will be mighty on earth; The generation of the upright will be blessed.

Psalm 112:2 AMP

We had just finished a week-long tent meeting outside of Charlotte, North Carolina. After we returned home, we started to notice my oldest daughter's health declining. Madelyn's fevers got worse, she lost her appetite entirely and stopped walking.

I finally made an appointment with a pediatrician. I thought it might have been a bad case of the flu, but it was worse. It's never reassuring when doctors run constant, frantic tests, but never say anything to you.

Finally, the primary doctor came back and said, "I believe she has a rare blood disease. I already called the Norfolk Children's Hospital and told them you'll be coming to the emergency room."

I went home to grab two things—my husband, Ted, and a bottle of oil. As soon as I pulled into the driveway, Ted came out and laid hands on her. In moments like this, when you receive a report that contradicts God's Word, you can accept it or prepare for battle. Ted and I were ready for a fight.

To make a long story short, in the hospital, we heard several reports—myocarditis, congestive heart failure, rheumatoid arthritis, and the list goes on. They saw fluid around Maddy's heart, she was in pain to the touch, and she wasn't walking, so they just gave me a long list of possibilities until they confirmed a blood disease.

Then, I received a list of things she wouldn't be able to do. This was my moment to either let compassion or faith take over. I watched my lifeless two-year-old beg her daddy to not let the nurses stick her with needles anymore as tears streamed down her face.

I left the room to pray. This was not going to be my daughter's story. If we were going to preach about Jesus, the healer, it would be true in our home first! This is one of the things for which Christ died. Jesus took my daughter's disease upon his body.

Fast forward, eight days. We never left her side. We prayed, we sang, and praised the Lord the entire time. They never gave her medication. After many daily tests, they reported that they couldn't find what they originally saw. *Hallelujah!* Just telling you this story makes me want to shout about God's goodness!

I gave you this testimony to show you that as a mother, I never let my love and compassion cloud my faith. It's not always easy, but it's a stance we are able to take. The same Jesus who keeps me healed is the same Jesus that keeps our children and grandchildren healed.

Keep that strength and fight the good fight of faith. Feed it regularly so it can grow.

PRAYER FOR TODAY

Thank you, Lord, for your continued strength. I will be full of faith when attacks come. I will stay in love but be strong and bold in my faith. I stand on Psalm 112:7: "They do not fear bad news; they confidently trust the Lord to take care of them."

DISCUSSION QUESTIONS

1. What does faith stronger than compassion look like?

2. Does this testimony make you remember one of your own? If you're in a group, share it with others. If you're alone, take time to praise and thank him for it.

3. How will you ensure your spirit is strong enough for battle?

4. What are some times in your own parenting where your faith needed to be stronger than compassion?

5. Does choosing faith over compassion show a lack of love? Why or why not?

DAY 18

CONFESSION

"I am generous to others around me."

The generous will prosper; those who refresh others will themselves be refreshed.

Proverbs 11:25 NLT

This is one of my favorite verses. Just think about a time you gave someone a gift. Think about how happy and excited you were to give it and how happy they were to receive it! Both giving and receiving brought joy. It brought refreshing, love, and happiness to the occasion.

I *love* to give! I am always finding an opportunity to give. It brings me great joy. Sometimes I think we overthink this process. We talk ourselves out of it. We think we can't afford to give all the time. Maybe we think the person we want to bless already has everything and needs nothing.

These are all lies of the enemy. Jesus has designed us to be sowers—not only with money but also with our time and talents. We all have something to give at some point.

Have you ever noticed that giving a compliment or a smile can break down a barrier? Whenever I encounter angry or frustrated people, I make a point to compliment them—their entire demeanor changes. People respond to kindness.

Gifts are always welcome. You don't have to spend a lot to make someone feel happy. Randomly giving a ten dollar bouquet of tulips, a Yankee Candle, or a cake to a friend makes room for you to speak into their lives.

The Bible says in Proverbs 18:16, "Giving a gift can open doors; it gives access to important people." You never know to whom you are being kind and generous. Being known as a giver represents Jesus well.

When Jesus was on the earth, people wanted to be around him. They flocked to him. He gave them wisdom, love, provision, miracles, food, and more. They knew him for being a giver, and that's what I want people to think of me. I challenge you today to do something unexpected for someone. The joyous feeling it brings is addictive—so get ready!

PRAYER FOR TODAY

Make me the biggest giver I can be to the kingdom and others around me. Let my giving open doors to talk about your goodness, and win more souls to Christ. Let my giving produce a harvest that gives me more seed to continue the cycle of giving in my life.

DISCUSSION QUESTIONS

1. Can you think of a time where a gift you gave made a greater impact on someone than you expected?

2. What about receiving? What is a gift you received that made a lasting impression? Why did it mean so much to you?

3. Who can you bless this month? How will your gift open the opportunity to impact their life for the kingdom?

4. Why does giving to others bring us joy and blessing ourselves?

5. What are some creative ways you can be a generous giver?

DAY 19

CONFESSION

"I will not let my joy be stolen. I will keep my joy intact, so that I can stay strong."

...Don't be dejected and sad, for the joy of the Lord is your strength.

Nehemiah 8:10 NLT

Keeping our joy and having joy is our choice. If we hand over our joy due to a bad report, what someone said, sinful actions, or if things aren't going our way, we end up giving the enemy an entrance into our lives.

Having supernatural joy is vital in our lives as believers. It sets the tone around us and is imparted to others— but it's even more important than that. It provides strength to our spirit.

How can we get through a situation when others wouldn't make it? Others would give up on their faith and open the door to the enemy. If we don't have the joy of the Lord, then we won't have the strength to stand in the face of adversity.

Sometimes I think we get the meaning of joy confused with happiness. Laughing is just an outward expression and can often be faked. Suicide is at an all-time high. The devil doesn't just want to steal your laughter; he wants your life (John 10:10). He'll go after your joy, and once you're in a weakened state, he'll be ready to pounce.

Have you ever heard that someone took their life and said, "They seemed so happy. I would never have thought they'd do something like this."

Joy comes from within. It's not surface level. Psalm 16:11 says, "You make known to me the path of life; you fill me with joy in your presence, with eternal pleasures at your right hand."

Do you see the key in that verse? In order to see your path of life and remain filled with joy along the way, you have to be in his presence at all times. We can not conjure up this type of joy by our power. It must come from one source—the Lord.

Staying in his presence is a requirement. You can't live in his presence and want to get drunk, stay depressed, want to sin, or have doubts about his Word. When we study and discover the truth within the pages of the Bible, we will have the joy of the Lord!

I'll leave you with two more verses: John 8:31-32. To

the Jews who had believed him, Jesus said, "If you hold to my teaching, you are really my disciples. Then you will know the truth, and the truth will set you free."

Stay in his presence by reading the Word, and your knowledge will always keep you one step ahead of the enemy and full of joy.

PRAYER FOR TODAY

Thank you, Lord, for filling me with power, faith, and determination. I am determined to read your Word. I am committed to staying in your presence so I can be strengthened and ready to defeat the enemy when he tries his tricks. My joy will not only be a blessing in my life but the lives of others. It will allow me to set people free from depression and bring more people into the kingdom.

DISCUSSION QUESTIONS

1. How will you cultivate an atmosphere of supernatural joy around you?

2. What are some things that steal joy? How many of those things do we have authority over?

3. The Bible says the joy of the Lord is our strength. Can you think of an experience where you saw this in action in your own life?

4. How will you share the joy of the Lord with someone this week?

5. What is your plan of action when a familiar feeling of sadness or fear tries to infiltrate your mind?

DAY 20

CONFESSION

"I declare that my entire household shall be saved."

Then he brought them out and asked, "Sirs, what must I do to be saved?" They replied, "Believe in the Lord Jesus and you will be saved, along with everyone in your household." And they shared the word of the Lord with him and with all who lived in his household.

Acts 16:30-32 NLT

We all have family members who need to hear the gospel. You should never give up on them, but pray that through you (or through someone else), they will hear the gospel and receive Jesus. The Holy Spirit can even soften the hearts of the family members we think are the hardest to reach.

People are searching for something real. There is so much that's fake in the world. That is why I stress being different than the world. No one will want to receive Jesus if we represent him poorly. Why on earth would they care to know my Jesus if serving him has no benefits?

Our lives need to be the best representation of Jesus possible. Sometimes, witnessing to family is the hardest because they have known us the longest, and maybe we didn't always serve the Lord. Maybe our family has a hard time forgetting who we used to be before salvation.

Don't let the past dictate your future or your soul-winning life. When you get saved, there needs to be a marked difference in your verbiage, how you conduct yourself, your prayer life, and your study life.

Though you may not always have the opportunity to speak to all of your family members, your life should be a testimony of what Christ has done in you. We are ambassadors of Heaven, and our actions need to represent that.

I'm believing with you today for your family. We have work to do! Be bold. Go after it and believe to see them in the kingdom. Time is running out. Jesus is coming soon. We don't want to stand before the Lord and regret missed opportunities. We want to know that what we did in this life was used to populate Heaven!

PRAYER FOR TODAY

Jesus, use me in these last days to be a bright light to my family. Give me boldness through your Holy Spirit. Please help me to obtain a revelation of your Word so I can stand out and live the way you planned. I will not go through what others go through. You set me free when you died on the cross and were raised from the dead. I want my family to be in Heaven with me, and I will work hard at getting them there.

DISCUSSION QUESTIONS

1. Who are you praying will receive salvation?

2. How is your life an example to them right now?

3. Is the Holy Spirit leading you in dealing with someone right now? How will you move forward?

4. What are some of the things salvation has given you?

5. Would you know these benefits of salvation if no one had ever shared them with you?

DAY 21

CONFESSION

"My children will be obedient. I will be mindful of discipline."

Children, obey your parents [as God's representatives] in all things, for this [attitude of respect and obedience] is well-pleasing to the Lord [and will bring you God's promised blessings].

Colossians 3:20 AMP

This can be a touchy subject, but it's so important we teach our children about discipline. We are doing a disservice to them if we don't teach them how to obey *and* the importance of obedience.

I grew up in a home with parents who weren't afraid to discipline me. Though no one likes discipline, I'm a better person for it. Now, as a parent, I see how God has entrusted us with children and expects us to raise them with his instructions.

Sometimes that involves spanking. Some parents may be afraid to discipline in this way because there have been cases of abuse. It's important to realize that abuse exists in every area of life. That doesn't mean we throw the baby out with the bathwater.

Proverbs 23:13-14 says, "Don't fail to discipline your children. The rod of punishment won't kill them. Physical discipline may well save them from death."

The dictionary defines discipline as "training which produces obedience or self-control, often in the form of rules and punishments if these are broken." Of course, the discipline the Bible talks about isn't abusive. On the other hand, it shouldn't be vague or inconsequential, leaving your child with no reason to change.

Our children were born with a sinful nature. When I discipline my children, it does hurt my heart, but I'm thinking of their future. Ephesians chapter 6 says my children will live a long life for obeying and honoring their parents. The blessings of God come to the obedient.

How can we expect our kids to obey someone they *can't* see if they won't obey their parents whom they *can* see? That will then bleed over into their school life with teachers, and eventually, their boss at a job.

This generation is easily offended, and when they don't get their way, they quit. We will disqualify our children from blessings God has for them if we don't do our part as parents. We discipline in love; we don't discipline in anger.

Proverbs 29:15 says, "To discipline a child produces wisdom, but a mother is disgraced by an undisciplined child."

PRAYER FOR TODAY

Thank you, Jesus, for the children you have given to me. I will work hard at being obedient to your Word, so my children will learn to be obedient to your Word. Give me the strength to discipline and teach them how to listen to me and you as well.

DISCUSSION QUESTIONS

1. How is discipline an intentional part of your parenting?

2. What does the Bible say about the necessity of obedience?

3. What are the rewards of obedience?

4. Are there any areas of inconsistency in the discipline and correction of your children? If so, what could improve?

5. Can you see any connections between the current state of the world and our culture and the lack of discipline in the home?

DAY 22

CONFESSION

"I am energetic and strong, but I don't have to do everything."

It is useless for you to work so hard from early morning until late at night, anxiously working for food to eat; for God gives rest to his loved ones.

Psalm 127: 2 NLT

Sometimes, we take on too many tasks, and then we become overwhelmed. We get cranky and snap at our friends, husbands, and kids. Then, we feel like we need to search for books on stress relief.

Let's pull back and look at the big picture. Were there things that I said yes to which I should have said no? Not everything that comes our way is something we need to do. Don't be pressured by the desire to make others happy by saying yes to everything.

Proverbs 31 shows us that women can do many things. We can take care of the home, family, and work hard without being overwhelmed and stressed. We can learn to balance and take on what is important in life. Sometimes we can fall prey to comparison, which becomes ugly and steals our joy and rest.

For example, if you have kids, have you ever had to provide snacks for their class? Some moms bring homemade cupcakes with picture-perfect icing and decorations . . . and we walk in with Twinkies from the local grocery store.

Both end up having the same result—happy kids who will eat them and never have another thought about it.

Why have a terrible night trying to make the best cupcakes ever when really you should have said no, and let someone else do it. I used to be the "yes person" wanting to please everyone until I realized I only had to please one person—Jesus. He wants to be involved in every detail of your life and wants you to have peace and rest in all that you do.

You can't be a good friend, wife, or mom if you're stressed out by your to-do list. Find things you can cut out of your schedule. Over the years, I've learned that just because you know how to do it all doesn't mean you should be doing it all.

PRAYER FOR TODAY

Thank you, Lord, for gifting me. Help me say yes to the right things and no to what I shouldn't be doing. I will find rest and joy in my decisions and focus on only pleasing you.

DISCUSSION QUESTIONS

1. Are there things to which you've said yes that need to be re-evaluated?

2. Do ungodly comparisons have any root in your life right now? What does the Bible say about comparison?

3. Is there an area of your life under unnecessary self-pressure? What can change?

4. What is your God-given purpose? Are your days filled with that purpose right now?

5. What does a stress-free day mean to you?

DAY 23

CONFESSION

"I will flourish in all seasons."

But if they delight in the law of the Lord, meditation on it day and night. They are like trees planted along the riverbank, bearing fruit each season. Their leaves never wither and they prosper in all they do.

Psalm 1:2-3 NLT

I dislike the false teaching that Christians have to have their ups and downs—our drought seasons. This teaching and thought process doesn't line up with the Word of God. I understand that Psalm 23 says we will walk through the valley of the shadow of death, but the problem is that some believers build a house in the valley instead of walking through it.

Then, we're forced to change our doctrine to accommodate these tragedies. No! Jesus has a plan to continually increase you. If you read Psalm 1, you will see that as we get the revelation of God's Word and spend time in his presence, our roots will grow strong and deep. We receive living water by studying the Word and obeying it. You cannot fail! You will prosper in all you do and in *every* season.

If you bear fruit in every season, that means your productivity will never lull. Your season may change, and the *type* of productivity may look different, but it will still be there. Just like seasons change, so does what we do, but each season has a purpose in its own way.

Find out what your purpose is when seasons change. Psalm 1 declares our leaves never wither, and we will prosper in all we do. Don't get caught up in the look of the season. The Bible says in Romans 8:14, "For all who are led by the Spirit of God are children of God." Ask the Lord what he wants you to do in this season.

PRAYER FOR TODAY

Lord, you have made me for a purpose. You have anointed me to be productive in all areas and in all seasons. My knowledge of the Word will increase and strengthen my roots, so my spirit man will never be weak. Your will is that I'm prosperous in all I do.

DISCUSSION QUESTIONS

1. Is it God's will to bring you through ups and downs? What does the Bible say?

2. Can you think of a time where others around you were experiencing loss or lack, but God sustained you supernaturally?

3. How will you maintain a strong spirit?

4. What does a productive day mean to you?

5. What specific areas of your life will prosper this month?

DAY 24

CONFESSION

"I'm not just a giver; I'm a receiver."

For the Lord God is our sun and our shield. He gives us grace and glory. The Lord will withhold no good thing from those who do what is right.

Psalm 84:11 NLT

Receiving is one thing we have to be very cautious about because it's the second half of God's system of seed-time and harvest. Everyone has been taught to give, but I find that people have a hard time receiving. We need to prepare ourselves to receive. We can't activate the first part of the covenant (giving) and not expect anything in return. It's just like breathing. We give a breath to receive another breath, and the cycle continues.

When the Lord speaks to me to bless someone financially, it's easier when they're prepared to receive. Apps like PayPal, Cash App, and Venmo allow me to sow instantly. (If you don't have an account like this, set one up today.)

Are we really ready to receive in 2020 if we aren't digitally prepared? I'll always keep my word to the Lord when he asks me to give, but it can get harder with life being busy. Who wants to hunt someone down to get their banking info or to mail a check? Be ready!

There are times I've asked kids what they want, and their answer is, "Nothing." I used to think it was sweet that the kids felt like they had everything until I really understood this principle.

We should be ready to answer when asked what we want. Not everything we receive has to meet a need. It's okay to want something and ask the Lord for it. He is a good father who wants to give good gifts to his children (Matthew 7:11). That's us. We are his children.

So now, I make a point to teach my kids to be ready at all times. We're training them to be givers *and* receivers. We're commanded in Philippians 4:6 to make our requests known unto God. That means he wants us to tell him what we want and expect to receive it.

Make a point to have an answer for someone and be prepared to receive. The Lord is looking for a way to bless you, and he will use a man or woman to do it. Get ready today!

PRAYER FOR TODAY

Thank you, Lord, for not only making me a big giver but making me a receiver. You want to bless me with more than spiritual blessings. You want to see my needs met *and* bless me with the things I want. I will learn to receive so I can walk in the fullness of my entire covenant.

DISCUSSION QUESTIONS

1. What is something specific you want the Lord to do for you today?

2. Have you struggled to be a receiver in the past? What does the Bible say about how we are to receive blessing?

3. What are three specific things you are believing the Lord to do for your family this year?

4. If God fully answered every single one of your prayers today, would you have all you wanted or have you not yet asked him?

5. How are you "set up to receive?"

DAY 25

CONFESSION

"God gave me the authority to guard my thoughts."

With these weapons we break down every proud argument that keeps people from knowing God. With these weapons we conquer their rebellious thoughts, and teach them, to obey Christ.

2 Corinthians 10:5 NLT

The Bible is very clear about how powerful our mind is and how we have authority over it. In several places, it tells us to keep our thoughts fixed on him to remain in perfect peace. He gave us a sound mind, and anything outside of that comes from the enemy.

Every negative thought blocks us from receiving our inheritance. It will stifle our faith. It makes us think we are unworthy to receive all that God has for us. It makes us feel we can't be powerful enough to carry out the plans of God.

Just like Paul instructed the Corinthians, we need to

rise up with authority and teach our rebellious thoughts to obey Christ. What does the Word say about you? What does the Word say about your situation? What you believe is eventually what you will say and become.

If we align our thinking with God's Word, when we speak, our confession will also be congruent with the Word of God. If your mind is focused on the truth, the supernatural will be at your command. Rise up in your authority and take control of your thoughts today!

PRAYER FOR TODAY

Lord Jesus, I take authority over any thoughts that don't come from you. I will capture carnal thoughts and make them obey Christ. You have a plan for me to carry out, and by knowing my identity in Christ, I can do it with boldness. I rebuke any lies from the enemy. His words don't line up with your Word. Your Word is the only truth I will believe.

DISCUSSION QUESTIONS

1. Are you believing any lies about your identity? What does the truth of God's Word say?

2. What thoughts you are taking authority over today?

3. How do you know if a thought is from God?

4. What is an area of your mind in which you have experienced personal freedom?

5. What are some ways to keep your thoughts aligned with the Word of God?

DAY 26

CONFESSION

"The love and intimacy in my marriage will continually increase."

This explains why a man leaves his father and mother and is joined his wife, the two reunited into one.

Genesis 2:24 NLT

I find this declaration very important because separations, divorce, and even infidelity are so prevalent in the Christian community. The enemy wants to destroy anything that represents unity. In unity, there is strength, and the devil wants to bring weakness.

As you see in the verse above, when you get married, you are joined together. There is instant unity when you stand at the altar. From that moment on, the enemy will try to squeeze his way in and separate you.

Staying intimate is something we should be working toward. I understand that as life gets busy with careers, kids, and age, we can get distracted and disregard intimacy with our spouse. We can get dangerously close to "roommate status."

God created intimacy. It's not a dirty word or something to feel ashamed of when you do it God's way.

Ladies, we can be famous for holding intimacy back due to our emotions. Anger, tiredness, and lack of confidence all come into play when we don't want to have sex. We use those tools to get out of it, but intimacy is an expression of love. It creates a tight bond between the two of you, and it guards against sexual sin. The Bible clearly instructs us not to hold it back and tells us why. (See 1 Corinthians 7:5 and Proverbs 5:15-17.)

We could come up with a million reasons why we don't have time for intimacy. Society will train you to put yourself, your career, and your kids first. But I got married to have a best friend, have an intimate relationship, form memories, and be a helpmate in his life as the Bible says I should.

We need to please our husbands, build them up, and make them feel loved and honored. Put away the excuses and watch how united you become by staying closer together in your relationship.

PRAYER FOR TODAY

Jesus, your Word says that what you join, no man can separate. I will put forth my best effort in preparing myself for my husband. I will be the best wife my husband could ever dream of. You made me beautiful and unique. I rebuke any lie from the enemy and any place he makes me feel inadequate in my calling as a wife. Thank you for joining me with my helpmate.

DISCUSSION QUESTIONS

1. How will true unity create strength in your marriage?

2. Are you aware of an area in your marriage that you have let slide over time? What action will you now take?

3. What is something unexpected you can do for your husband today that will make him feel loved and honored?

4. How will you better prioritize intimacy in your marriage?

5. Is there any area of unforgiveness that you have let fester in your relationship? What does the Bible say about harboring unforgiveness?

DAY 27

CONFESSION

"I will not let offense hinder my blessing."

Good sense makes one slow to anger, and it is his glory to overlook an offense.

Proverbs 19:11 ESV

Can you imagine being called a dog or feeling like you're unworthy to receive but so desperate to speak out? Let me set this up for you. The story of the Gentile woman in Matthew 15 speaks volumes about looking beyond an offense to receive your miracle.

Gentiles were not "God's people." Jesus explains to her that he was sent to God's children. If you look at verses 26 and 27, Jesus explains that he shouldn't be focusing on people outside of Israel and calls Gentiles dogs.

I know you may think that was harsh of Jesus. I hate to break it to you, Jesus wasn't a pansy who roamed the earth hugging everyone. Although his message was one of love, he spoke with strength, authority, and kindness. The moment he answered the Gentile woman, it could have gone two ways. She could have stood up, yelled at him, and ran away. Instead, she was a smart woman who made a very wise move.

Her response was, "But even dogs are permitted to eat crumbs that fall beneath the master's table." *Wow!* She had every opportunity to be offended, but that would have disqualified her from receiving the miracle she wanted.

Staying in a state of offense will knock you out of what God has for you. Can you take correction? Correction is just direction for your life. Can you handle someone giving you parenting tips, or would you consider that criticism of your parenting skills? You can choose whether or not to be offended. The ball is now in your court.

One way to avoid offense is to be free from seeking the approval of others. It's easy to over-prioritize the opinions of others. Just like the Gentile woman. The disciples wanted to send her away. They criticized her, and Jesus ignored her. However, she didn't care what she looked like. She had one thing in mind—her daughter's miracle.

Make decisions based upon instructions from the Lord and never apologize for them. Stick with what you've been told, and don't worry about what others have to say. People will always throw "suggestions" at you, but the real instruction for your life always comes from the Lord. Only seek his approval. When you're grounded in your heavenly identity, you can avoid being offended and stay on track with what God has instructed you to do.

PRAYER FOR TODAY

Thank you, Jesus, that you give me the ability to overlook offense. I will not let the words of others trip me up and knock me out of God's blessings. I am open to correction because you only want the best for me.

DISCUSSION QUESTIONS

1. Can you describe a time when someone's correction provided a life-changing turn of direction for you?

2. What does the Bible say about taking offense?

3. Can you recognize any root of offense that you have been holding on to?

4. How does seeking the approval of man over the approval of God bring destruction in your life?

5. What does choosing to reject offense do in your life?

DAY 28

CONFESSION

"My thankfulness is a spiritual shield against unbelief, self-sufficiency, and discontentment."

Let them praise the Lord for his great love and wonderful things he has done for them.

Psalm 107:31 NLT

Lately, my girls and I have created a nightly routine. We've been watching different Bible stories before bed. We get to discuss what is going on and watch how people used to live. As Americans, my kids don't know what it means to be persecuted for serving Jesus. This is something they see a lot as we watch stories from the New Testament.

One example is the Apostle Paul. He had a major change in his life after his experience on the road to Damascus. People remained suspicious of him because of his violent reputation.

Despite the abuse he went through, he learned the true meaning of thanksgiving. Paul encouraged the Ephesians to give thanks while he was imprisoned (Eph 5:20). Some people lose their joy if they forget their lunch and have to buy a vending machine snack at work.

Don't wait until Thanksgiving Day to be thankful. It needs to be a daily reality in our lives that turns us into joyful people. To me, being thankful for all that God has done in your life should be a distinctive mark of a Christian. We don't want bitterness, selfishness, or discontentment to steal our joy, faith, fullness of healing, or our peace.

Look at the story of Jesus healing the ten lepers in Luke 17:11-19. Even though Jesus healed them all, only one returned to give thanks. We know what leprosy does to the body. It not only kills you, but it also disfigures your body and cuts you out of society.

All ten were healed of the disease, but nine were so preoccupied with themselves that a spirit of ingratitude took over, and they weren't thankful. The one who returned to give thanks was made whole. I believe Jesus made this man look like he never even had the disease at all

When you get to the point of ungratefulness, you live dangerously on the line of sin. I know it sounds harsh, but look at what Romans 1:21 says: "Yes, they knew God, but they wouldn't worship him as God or even give him thanks. And they began to think up foolish ideas of what God was like. The result was their minds became dark and confused."

An ungrateful heart is a heart that is cold towards God and has forgotten how dependent we are on our Savior.

Each day, I make a point to thank the Lord. Every night before bed, I prompt my children to list one thing for which they are thankful. We teach them that everything we have comes from the Lord.

If you follow Psalm 147:7 by always having a song of thanksgiving, the enemy can't knock you out of staying in a continual state of receiving. I want everything the Lord has for me, and I know you do, too.

PRAYER FOR TODAY

I will make a habit of singing songs and giving thanks to the Lord. I will set the tone for my surroundings. I will continually praise him for his greatness and stay thankful for my blessings and answers to my prayers. Thank you, Lord, for doing so much for me. You're always working for me even when I don't see it all. I'll never stop being thankful.

DISCUSSION QUESTIONS

1. How does it make you feel when someone is ungrateful? Would you want God to feel that way?

2. Have you cultivated a spirit of thankfulness in your life and home? How so?

3. What are the benefits of having a thankful heart?

4. What was the last thing you thanked God for?

5. If you weren't saved, and if you did not know the goodness of God in your life, where would you be today?

DAY 29

CONFESSION

"I will never know what it is to retreat. I only advance."

The name of the Lord is a strong tower; the righteous run to it and are safe.

Proverbs 18:10 ESV

We tend to forget how much power we have as believers. What Jesus did on the cross was crucial because once he rose from the dead and ascended to Heaven, the Holy Spirit was sent who gave us power. We don't ever have to lose to the devil (Luke 10:19). We have *all* power!

The Bible tells us we are in the army of the Lord. What does that mean? It means to be ready for battle. Can you imagine our military never knowing how to fight, shoot a gun, or defend us in a war? They are trained from the moment they attend boot camp. They are whipped into shape, vigilant, and prepared to win. They don't just look the part; they act the part.

If you read Ephesians 6:10-17, you'll see that we

should be wearing the armor of God. We don't wake up and choose one piece to wear each day. We are supposed to fully dress ourselves every day. Each piece is essential during an attack.

No matter how the enemy attacks you, the armor makes you ready to win the battle. We're never to run away from the enemy; we're supposed to charge the enemy!

The Lord hasn't just equipped us for battle, but he is also protecting his children. Psalm 32:7 says, "For you are my hiding place; you protect me from trouble, You surround me with songs of victory."

God has given us all the proper tools *plus* a place to hide. We are protected on every side and set up to win. Don't give up. Don't give the enemy an entrance into your life. Stand up for what Christ accomplished on the cross.

Do you want healing? Do you want peace in your home? You want to be free from addiction and shame? Do you want a good marriage? Don't believe the commonly-uttered phrase, "you can't have your cake and eat it too." You can have it all.

We are supposed to live victoriously. We are joint heirs with Christ. My weapons carry divine power to demolish anything the enemy sends to destroy me!

PRAYER FOR TODAY

Jesus, I thank you that you have given me everything I need to win every battle. I live a victorious, overcoming life. The enemy has no power. I rebuke every enemy trying to gain entrance into my life. I receive the revelation of what it means to be more than a conqueror. You took all the physical punishment so I could be strong enough to fight the supernatural fight. Thank you for making me strong!

DISCUSSION QUESTIONS

1. What area in your life are you conquering today?

2. What does being a powerful Christian mean to you?

3. Has God ever been defeated in battle? Has he called you to be?

4. How do you prepare yourself as a "soldier" for the Lord?

5. What part of your own daily routine builds your spirit man?

DAY 30

CONFESSION

"My loyalty is shown by my commitment."

Understand therefore, that the Lord your God is indeed God. He is the faithful God who keeps his covenant for a thousand generations and constantly loves those who love him and obey his commands.

Deuteronomy 7:9 NLT

The definition of loyalty is a strong feeling of support or allegiance. What comes to mind when we hear the word loyalty? Our job? Our spouse? Our faith? Loyalty affects how we approach life. Will it be God's way or the world's way?

Sometimes when we don't see the big picture, we have to depend on our faith and make up our minds that no matter what, we know where our loyalties lie. Many are loyal to their natural commitments, but what about our supernatural responsibilities? I'm going to be asking a lot of questions in this devotional because we need to become introspective and examine our loyalties. Lip service is easy. It's our actions that prove our dedication.

Loyalty means a sincere devotion of the heart. Does Jesus hold the highest place in your heart? What are some ways you prove that to him? Do you spend time talking to him? Do you get to know his nature by reading the Word?

There are two different types of Christians. Some operate in the fullness of God's Word, and there are Christians who ignore it. Some live by faith, and others barely live due to their lack of knowledge. Both are going to Heaven but will see very different results on the earth.

Loyalty makes us active. If you are loyal to someone, you'll follow their advice. Look at the disciples after Jesus ascended. They were loyal to his teaching and carried out the commands of their Master. (See Mark 16:15-20.)

There comes a time when we stop being a "prayer project," grow in God's things, and lay our hands on the sick and watch them recover.

Loyalty causes us to be obedient and to show honor. For example, every Christian should attend church faithfully. We shouldn't put anything else first. We shouldn't miss church for a vacation, a sports event, or anything else we could be doing. We can never make light of anything the Word of God commands us to do. (See Hebrews 10:25.)

A lifestyle of loyalty to the Word of God will result in the benefits that accompany obedience. God's way is always higher than the way of men (Isaiah 55:8-9).

PRAYER FOR TODAY

I am a believer that is loyal to the ways of God. I follow his truth. I understand his nature, and I'm committed to his ways no matter what. I have a genuine love for him and his instructions.

DISCUSSION QUESTIONS

1. What does a life without loyalty bring?

2. What benefits does loyalty bring to your life?

3. What are you most committed to in your life? How do you prioritize the things of God on a daily basis?

4. How is loyalty seen specifically in your lifestyle?

5. How will you teach the principle of loyalty to your children?

DAY 31

CONFESSION

"Jesus takes sickness far from me."

But he was pierced for our rebellion, crushed for our sins. He was beaten so we could be whole. He was whipped so we could be healed.

Isaiah 53:5 NLT

The topic of healing is one of my favorites. I've always been drawn to learning about it. As I grew up, I realized how important it is to truly understand what the Bible says about healing so that we don't change our doctrine to accommodate tragedies.

Obviously, we will know Christians who die because of sicknesses or diseases. Understand that being a Christian alone isn't enough to receive all that God has for you. Some Christians understand the blessings they'll experience in Heaven, but don't know they can obtain heavenly blessings while they're still on the earth.

Christians need this revelation. We must understand our heavenly Father's nature and believe and speak his

Word. If we're not well-grounded in this area, it will be easy for the enemy to come and steal (John 10:10), and tell us lies that we'll gladly believe. Studying and standing in faith is our responsibility.

One of my favorite stories of healing in the Bible is the women with the issue of blood in Mark 5:25-34. This woman suffered for twelve years. She tried everything but faith. She finally pursued the anointing of Christ.

This woman even went broke because of years of medical expenses. Notice how a lack of healing also affected her financially. Living in divine healing can positively affect many areas of life: finances, joy, relationships, etc.

Even though she made Jesus her last option, he still acknowledged her faith. He felt her reach out and touch him. She grabbed ahold of the healing power that was in him, and it left his body.

Jesus didn't rebuke her for grabbing his clothes; he responded by calling her daughter. Our heavenly Father is a healer; it's part of his nature. He doesn't make us suffer. He doesn't cause sickness in our lives. Would an earthly (imperfect) father force his kids to suffer from sickness? No. Nor does your perfect heavenly Father use sickness to make you suffer.

We can't properly work for the Lord and be his witnesses if we are immobilized by constant pain and sickness.

Even though Jesus is always willing to heal, don't make him your last option. She didn't have to lose all of her money and suffer for twelve years. Isaiah 58:8-9 says God will quickly reply and heal you.

Choose to stand in faith today. Deposit the Word of God in your heart so that it continually flows out of you. Faith comes by hearing (Romans 10:17). I'm not just talking about hearing ministers preach. You should also hear your voice speaking faith.

God won't rebuke you for asking for healing. He's waiting to take care of his children. He loves you so much and wants you to be healed while here on earth. It's your right as a believer. Don't settle for less!

PRAYER FOR TODAY

Thank you, Jesus, for taking care of me. I know you want to see me walk in healing. I rebuke the enemy for any lies that have tried to enter my thoughts to make me believe otherwise. I command sickness, pain, and disease to leave my body. They are trespassing. I command every organ to function correctly and every cell to line up correctly. Anything that doesn't belong in my bloodstream must quickly dissolve.

DISCUSSION QUESTIONS

1. How do you know that divine healing is your right as a child of God?

2. What are some of the ways that God takes care of you as your father?

3. Have you ever been desperate for a miracle like the woman with the issue of blood? What is it about her faith that stands out to you?

4. What verses show us that Jesus takes *all* sickness far from us and not just some?

DAY 32

CONFESSION

"God's anointing resides in my home."

The Lord shall increase you more and more, you and your children.

Psalm 115:14 KJV

2 Kings 4:8-37 is a compelling story that shows great strength from a woman who had experienced a tragedy. This woman from Shunem built a room in her home for the prophet Elisha. Any time he came through town, she had a comfortable place for him to stay.

Elisha found out that she wanted a son but wasn't able to have a baby. God blessed her with the ability to have a baby for taking care of the prophet.

Later, as her child became older and was working out in the field, he felt pain in his head and died. Her first thought was to carry him up to the prophet's room and lay him on the bed. After she did, she saddled a donkey and went to find Elisha.

She then begged Elisha to return to the house and help her son. Elisha did as the woman asked, and when he got to the house, he stretched himself out on the boy's body until he came back to life.

I want you to read the full story, but there are some key points I want to show you. You can declare, "My home is where the anointing resides," and see it come to pass.

First, we see Elisha as an anointed man of God. The woman saw that and made room in her house for him. She knew the importance of having the anointing in her home. Elisha was anointed, and he represented the anointing.

Next, she received an answer to prayer through her devotion to the anointing. In Isaiah 10:27, the Bible says that the anointing breaks every yoke of bondage. Bondage is a restraint that holds us back. Staying in the anointing destroys the enemy's plans allowing us to obtain God's promises.

When the woman's son died, she didn't accept it. She rode off to bring the prophet home for help. She knew God's power was stronger than death.

One of my favorite parts of this story was when she met Elisha's servant and he asked if everything was okay, her response was, "Yes, everything is fine." All she could think about was her dead son, but she answered in complete peace and faith. How would you have responded? She stayed focused and determined that the anointing would provide peace during a tragic time, and everything was going to be alright.

The Shunnamite woman was not satisfied with her bad report, and we aren't to be either. What bad report have you received recently? Don't accept it! Find out what God's Word says about it. Truth trumps facts.

Death may be trying to touch our marriage, relationships with our children, friendships, finances, joy, or our bodies because of sickness and disease.

Don't become satisfied when an answer comes that is against what you have confessed. Make room for the anointing in your house. Let it fill your marriage, home, body, and mind.

PRAYER FOR TODAY

I will make sure I have the anointing of God in my home. I rebuke any bad reports in the name of Jesus. I will believe the report of the Lord. The enemy has no say in my life. I will align my confession with the truth of God's Word. No matter what the situation looks like, I believe the anointing destroys anything that's not from God. In the anointing, there is peace, healing, and restoration in my atmosphere.

DISCUSSION QUESTIONS

1. How will you make room for the anointing in your home?

2. Is there a situation in your life right now that needs to line up with what the Word of God says?

3. What does an anointed home mean to you?

4. What is your plan of action if a situation arises in your home or family that contradicts what the Word says?

5. What are you believing God to do in your home this week?

DAY 33

CONFESSION

"My children will be mighty on the earth. The generation of the upright is blessed."

Children born to a young man are like arrows in a warrior's hands.

Psalm 127:4 NLT

As parents, we have a job—raising godly children. I believe it's the most important job you can have. No one else has authority over your children; it has been given to you. He gave us the anointing and grace to parent them in a godly way.

We must take the time to deposit the Word of God into them at a young age. Our children are called to be mighty warriors. It is our job to continually train them, which is an everyday job. (See Proverbs 22:6.)

We started a kids ministry called Miracle Word Kids. One of the primary purposes is to encourage kids to read the Bible, learn to pray, and get revelation and wisdom at a young age. I want children to see deeper things in the Word. One of the verses we use as our theme for the kids' ministry is Luke 2:40, "There the child grew up healthy and strong. He was filled with wisdom, and God's favor was on him."

I love reading verses 41 through 52. They show Jesus as a young boy hungry to learn about godly things. He was sitting in the temple with the religious leaders, asking questions, and gaining knowledge.

The more revelation of the Scriptures you gain, the more hungry you become. Although Jesus was born a King (the son of God), he didn't go around acting that way.

As a child, he remained teachable and was training for his upcoming ministry. The Bible tells us that all who heard him were amazed at his answers and understanding. That is how we produce mighty kids. We must continuously fill them with the Word.

PRAYER FOR TODAY

Thank you, Lord, for entrusting me with my children. Continue to anoint me to raise them in a way that's pleasing to you. Open their eyes to see the powerful truths of your Word, and use them mightily to touch their generation.

DISCUSSION QUESTIONS

1. What are some of the ways you can teach your children the Word of God?

2. What does your prayer time as a family currently look like? Could anything be better?

3. How are you stewarding your authority and responsibility as a parent?

4. What is one verse you are standing on as a parent right now?

5. What does having "mighty children" mean to you?

DAY 34

CONFESSION

"I will continually praise God for his greatness."

Let everything that has breath sing praises to the Lord.

Psalm 150:6 NLT

We must live with an attitude of praise toward God. We can allow lots of things to steal praise from our lives. I understand praise isn't always easy, but Hebrews 13:5 calls praise a sacrifice. Despite our feelings or circumstances, we have to take the first step. It's the fastest access into the presence of God.

We force ourselves to do things we don't always feel like doing. We don't always feel like getting out of bed to go to work, driving our kids around to all of their activities, or making dinner each night for everyone, but we do it anyway.

We don't praise God based on our feelings; we praise him because of who he is and what he has done for us.

He is worthy of our praise. He is the Alpha and Omega, the beginning and the end, the King of kings, our healer, provider, deliverer, defender, just to name a few.

Do you need a miracle? We don't praise God after we receive a miracle; that's when we give thanks. Praise is done before we see what we need. Jesus can work miraculously through our praise.

Think back to the walls of Jericho. Praising and shouting alone brought down the walls. What about Paul and Silas? They were in no position to praise. They were sitting in a cold, damp, and dirty cell, and chained to a wall. Why would they think to praise God?

They never took their circumstances into account. You have to make up your mind to praise when your life looks great or if it doesn't. Not only did their praise provide protection, but it also gave them (and the rest of the prisoners) freedom.

Not only did it provide protection and freedom, but it also provided salvation to the guard. Our praise is a powerful witness to those who don't know the Lord. Three major things happened all because Paul and Silas were obedient to the instructions of God. Psalm 150:6 doesn't say, "Let everything that has breath praise the Lord if things are going well." It simply says if you have breath, then you are to praise the Creator.

If we follow the Word of God's instruction in Psalm 34:1, "I will praise the Lord at all times. I will constantly speak his praises," we will have no room for negative confessions. If you're continually speaking the Word and giving glory and honor to Jesus, that's a sure way to maintain the correct confession. The enemy can't slip something in if you stay in a constant state of praise.

Take a moment now and speak audibly to the Lord. Tell him how wonderful he is for all that he has done. Whether you feel like you can or not, do it anyway. It will turn your attention away from your problems and onto the nature and character of God.

I make a point to blast praise music continually, dance around the kitchen with my wooden spoon microphone, and get my kids involved. It brings such joy to the atmosphere. I encourage you to try. There's only one outcome.

PRAYER FOR TODAY

I will learn to praise you through every situation. Praising pushes me out of the valley and into the goodness of God. Thank you for all that you have done for me and all you will do for my family and me.

DISCUSSION QUESTIONS

1. What is something you are praising and thanking God for ahead of time right now?

2. List at least five things God has blessed you with today and thank him for them!

3. How will your home be a home that is always filled with praise? What are some practical things you can do?

4. Can you think of a time in your life when you didn't feel like praising, but upon doing so, your breakthrough came?

5. Who is God to you today? Tell him!

DAY 35

CONFESSION

"My spirit of faith says, 'I believe, so I speak.'"

I tell you the truth, you can say to this mountain, may you be lifted up and thrown into the sea, and it will happen. But you must really believe it will happen and have no doubt in your heart.

Mark 11:23 NLT

This principle is what this whole book is about—believing and speaking. Declaring, declaring, declaring! It seems like some people place more faith in what others say than the Word. We are too easily persuaded. If what someone tells me doesn't line up with the Word, I automatically reject it. Anything that discourages our faith is a trap from the enemy.

In Matthew 17:20, the Bible says if we have faith the size of a mustard seed, we can move a mountain. Think about that. Something that small can move something that big.

What if we took that tiny seed and watered it daily so it could grow? Then what would we have faith to do? I know it's not a popular message, but there are different levels of faith. Don't start thinking you'll never be where someone else is. We are all given the chance and responsibility to grow.

There are several places where Jesus rebuked his disciples for their lack of faith. You can have little faith, and you can have great faith. The Word of God shows us we can be at different levels.

I want to encourage you that you don't have to stay at your current level. We are called to level up. We are supposed to go from faith to faith, glory to glory, and strength to strength. Faith will take us out of our comfort zone. Here's why: if we remain comfortable, we won't move.

How will we go from faith to faith if we remain comfortable? Don't settle in where you are. It's great you have been victorious in the past, but don't get stagnant. That word means to become stale or foul from standing.

Don't stop developing, growing, progressing, or advancing. That is exactly what the enemy wants you to do. If there is no growth, there is no life. If there is no life, you will not be speaking. Dead people don't talk.

You have to press in for what's greater. Keep your heart in faith. Keep the right confession in your mouth. If the

Bible declares *all* things are possible, we should realize all means 100%. We can't allow life experience to determine what we believe. If what we see contradicts the Word, shut it down. Our belief and speaking go hand in hand. In Mark 11:22-24, Jesus commands his disciples to have the God kind of faith.

Remember, faith is an action word. We must work it. Don't stay stagnant or comfortable at your current level. There is no cap on our faith. We should continuously increase in every area of the Word!

PRAYER FOR TODAY

Thank you, Jesus, that I have great faith! Faith that can do whatever your Word says I can. I will not remain at my current level. Even if I feel like I have great faith now, I always have the opportunity to go higher. I want to go higher. Thank you for making me bold and for allowing me to increase in every area of my walk with you.

DISCUSSION QUESTIONS

1. What is something outside of your comfort zone that faith has required of you?

2. How will you be a person of strong faith?

3. What will keep you moving forward in faith so that you never stagnate?

4. What does the next level of faith look like to you?

5. Is there anything in your thoughts that needs correction because it contradicts the Word of God?

DAY 36

CONFESSION

"The path of my life will be determined by God, not man."

The Lord says I will guide you along the best pathway for your life. I will advise you and watch over you.

Psalm 32:8 NLT

Isn't it wonderful that we never have to go through life wondering what we are supposed to do, who we should marry, what school to attend, where to live, what job to take, or what house to buy? These are major decisions we have to make throughout life.

The older I get, the more I realize that I don't have to make those decisions. This is where prayer and fasting come into play. We need to stay in tune with the Spirit so we can listen to him.

There's an old hymn that I sing to myself. It's very simple, yet so powerful. The words are "Trust and obey because there's no other way to be happy in Jesus but to trust and obey."

That is the key. To discover the path he has for us, we have to trust and obey. The Holy Spirit can't lead us if we feel like we have to be the leader. On a tour, we don't tell the tour guide where to go. We are there to be led.

We also may have to let go of some relationships. Not everyone is called to go where we are going. Our attachment to certain people can lead us down the wrong path. I don't always mean a path of sin and worldly actions, but if it's not the course for you, it won't be a smooth journey.

During construction, scaffolding is used while the structure is being built. Afterward, the scaffolding isn't meant to remain. Some people in our life aren't meant to go where we are going. They are there for a season, and then, as you continue in the direction you are supposed to go, some will fall away.

Don't be broken-hearted or discouraged. Focus on the good things God has planned out for you (Jeremiah 29:11). Focus on the rewards for trusting and obeying the Word of God. People will always come and go, but the Word of God will remain the same forever.

Ask the Lord to reveal your path to you. Are you on the one he has for you? Do you have the right people in your life? Find out today.

PRAYER FOR TODAY

Thank you, Jesus, that I hear your voice. Every decision will be the right decision because your Spirit leads me. I'll never wander through life, wondering why things aren't working out. I'll succeed through my dedication to being led by you.

DISCUSSION QUESTIONS

1. If someone were to ask you what your purpose is, could you answer them with confidence?

2. Is there anything in your life you can see is hindering your purpose? If so, what action will you take?

3. Are your relationships adding to your purpose, or holding you back from going to the next level?

4. Is there a decision in your life that requires fasting and prayer this week?

5. What doors are you believing God to open next to fulfill your purpose?

DAY 37

CONFESSION

"My revelation of God's Word allows me to pull his promises into the natural realm."

Open for me the gates where the righteous enter, and I will go in and thank the Lord.

Psalm 118:19 NLT

Do you ever look at people during a crisis and wonder why they are not freaking out? What makes them so calm? I often have people say that to me. I've been told to check my pulse during stressful situations over the years.

When people first started pointing this out about me, I began to think, "Is something wrong with me? Am I broken? Do I not have feelings?" As I began to ask the Lord about it, he reassured me that I was perfectly fine. He told me that it's caused by having revelation of his Word.

When you receive revelation of the Word, your faith leaps. When we speak these declarations, it makes us see the victory that Jesus won on our behalf. When you receive revelation of the Word, you become bold and confident.

As doors began to open for me to speak, I wanted my messages to come from revelation of his Word. When my spirit man can see it, I can minister from the unction of the Holy Spirit. I can see what the Word is saying, and I desire to operate in it.

I love Daniel 11:32. It says, "But the people that know their God shall be strong and will do exploits." Let me emphasize—people that *know* their God. What do you know about your heavenly Father? Have you studied his nature or what he wants for you?

It becomes a lot easier to spread the gospel when you are confident about your resources and what you've been sent to do. What do confidence and boldness do? They give us the backbone to conquer our enemy. He has no power. The only power he has is the power we give him.

There is nothing to fear about the enemy. The Bible says he goes around *like* a roaring lion. When you receive revelation of the Word, you stay in a constant state of supernatural peace. Don't let circumstances move you.

John chapter 14 tells us that peace was a gift given to us by Jesus. The world has no right to take it. The world didn't give it to us. Be a person that is never anxious. Don't allow yourself to be disturbed. Be the calm in the storm.

Psalm 119:165 says, "Those who love your instructions have great peace and do not stumble." You can be fully confident in your rest.

There are levels in revelation. You must never stop increasing your knowledge of Scripture. I once heard Dr. David Oyedepo say, "The level of our revelation determines our degree of dominion." I will never forget it. That is such an eye-opener!

If you don't like what is going on in your life, change it by gaining new levels of scriptural truth. Make time for dedicated study and set your faith on the revelation that you receive. God has given us all the resources we need to adequately confront any struggles.

Revelation gives us victory over the enemy, but it also keeps us in a place of joy, divine healing, prosperity, and more! The more we know, the better off we will always be.

PRAYER FOR TODAY

Thank you, Jesus, for giving me life's manual. As a believer, I don't have to be confused about my inheritance. Your Word is alive, powerful, and able to guide me. I will take the time to study Scripture. You've already done all the work. I will now take responsibility and do my part.

DISCUSSION QUESTIONS

1. Do you live your life in a state of constant supernatural peace? If not, what is the Lord showing you to change?

2. What are some of the resources God has made available to you in his Word?

3. What great exploits has God called you to do?

4. Can you think of a personal revelation of God's Word that made a crucial impact on your life?

5. How do you best combat feelings of anxiety or worry?

DAY 38

CONFESSION

"God is always willing to help me"

Jesus reached out and touched him. "I am willing," he said. "Be healed!" And instantly the leprosy disappeared.

Matthew 8:3 NLT

I often think about the verse above because I hear a lot of Christians say, "If it be God's will." So what is God's will? Sometimes we say things that sound good or share catchy quotes online because they're written with a pretty font or a well-designed graphic, but do they really line up with the Word of God? Is the will of God a roll of the dice? Does he sometimes have a great plan for us and other times he leaves us hanging out to dry?

How can we read the Bible and think it has changed? Jesus told the lepers "I am willing," then proceeded to heal them. Jesus was not double minded and never will be. We shouldn't be double minded either.

Romans 12:2 commands us, "Don't copy the behavior

and customs of this world, but let God transform you into a new person by changing the way you think. Then you will learn to know God's will for you, which is good, pleasing, and perfect." Go back and read that verse again and find out how many different wills God has for your life. How many did you find? One.

So Jesus is *always* willing to save, heal, restore, provide, and show his goodness to his children. We aren't to look at the situations of others and change the Word of God to fit the circumstances. On the contrary, the Word of God will change the circumstances. God answers with fire and authority. (See 1 Kings 18.) That fire consumes what doesn't belong in our lives.

So from this point on, it's important to know the true nature of who we serve. It's important to know God's will for our lives. It's important to know how to pray and stand in faith until our miracle comes to pass.

Just because we don't see Jesus working instantly doesn't mean he's not working constantly. Jesus died so we can live in his perfect will for our lives. Don't dismiss your promise with cute sayings that feel good to your flesh. Instead of praying, "If it be your will," say, "Lord, I know you are willing!"

PRAYER FOR TODAY

Jesus, show me your will for my life. I know you have one that's specific to me. I will be obedient to your instructions. I refuse to doubt your unchanging goodness. Anything that isn't good is from the devil (John 10:10). Today, I receive your promises by faith.

DISCUSSION QUESTIONS

1. How can you be confident that it's always God's will to heal?

2. Is there ever an exception to God's willingness or desire to heal you?

3. Is there anything in your life that "isn't good" and therefore isn't God's will for you to have?

4. How can you stop circumstances from defining what you believe?

5. What are some of the promises God has given you in his Word?

DAY 39

CONFESSION

"I can see what others can't see because the Lord has opened my spiritual eyes."

Then Elisha prayed and said, "O Lord, please open his eyes that he may see." So the Lord opened the eyes of the young man, and he saw, and behold, the mountain was full of horses and chariots of fire all around Elisha.

2 Kings 6:17 ESV

"If I would have known that ahead of time, my decision would have been different." Have you ever had that thought? By seeing into the supernatural realm, we can know things ahead of time. The Bible tells us that we are not a part of this world. By not being a part of it we can know things by the Holy Spirit's voice by looking through spiritual eyes. You can go further by walking according to what you see in the spirit rather than the natural. Your faith will be activated by the Spirit's vision.

I want to show you two different types of vision. First,

look at the story of Elijah and Elisha in 2 Kings 2. Elisha served the prophet Elijah. His service to the anointing gave him the ability to see like his master.

My father-in-law, Ted Shuttlesworth Sr., always says, "You have to sit under a gift to receive a gift." Serving is the key to impartation.

Elijah tells Elisha, "If you see me when I go, you will get your request of a double portion of my spirit." That's exactly what happened. As soon as the chariot of fire and angels came down to carry Elijah to Heaven, Elisha saw it. That was a supernatural event and proof he already had spiritual vision.

His desire for the anointing and his service gave him access to impartation and spiritual vision. Elijah didn't have to pray for him; Elisha just saw into the spirit realm.

In 2 Kings 6, Elisha has become the prophet and Gehazi is his servant. They had been surrounded by the Arameans. When Gehazi woke up and left the tent, he saw army, and fear gripped him instantly.

Natural vision.

In a panic, he ran back and reported to his master. Elisha didn't even have to leave the tent to give his response to Gehazi. He said, "Do not be afraid, for those who are with us are more than those who are with them." Then, Elisha prayed and said, "O Lord, please open his eyes that he may see."

The Lord opened Gehazi's eyes. He saw that the mountain was full of horses and chariots of fire all around them.

Elisha had to pray for Gehazi to have spiritual vision because he wasn't walking by the Spirit. Gehazi never became a prophet and was overtaken by greed because he only looked at the natural realm. (See 2 Kings 5.)

You have two sets of eyes—spiritual and natural. With prophetic vision can see what other people can't see. God wants to show you things ahead of time so you're never taken off guard. (See Jeremiah 33:3.)

Elisha was able to take over Elijah's ministry because of his vision and impartation. The same is true for you as a believer. We are called to take over the ministry of Jesus (John 14:12).

You will never be destroyed by the secret plans of the enemy when you have prophetic vision. You don't have to go through the crises of this world. Supernatural vision is not just for ministers, it can be received by every believer.

It's time to live in the image of our Savior. We are the only hope for this world. We have the answer to the world's problems.

PRAYER FOR TODAY

Open my eyes to your Word, Lord. I want to know what you have for me before the enemy tries to attack me. I want to see what you see. I want to walk in the anointing and plan you have for my life. Use me to help people out of their problems by showing me the plans you have.

DISCUSSION QUESTIONS

1. How do you see into the supernatural?

2. Have you sat under any gifts? Can you see them working in your life because you did?

3. Can you think of a time in your life when your eyes were opened to the supernatural realm behind your current circumstance?

4. When you look at circumstances with natural vision only, what does it prevent you from experiencing?

5. Has God given you a promise that you are waiting to see in the natural? How will you keep your supernatural vision in focus?

DAY 40

CONFESSION

"I have divine rights."

"You shall therefore lay up these words of mine in your heart and in your soul, and you shall bind them as a sign on your hand, and they shall be as frontlets between your eyes. You shall teach them to your children, talking of them when you are sitting in your house, and when you are walking by the way, and when you lie down, and when you rise. You shall write them on the doorposts of your house and on your gates, that your days and the days of your children may be multiplied in the land that the Lord swore to your fathers to give them, as long as the heavens are above the earth."

Deuteronomy 11:18-21 ESV

Jesus wants us to live at our full potential as his children. We should look different than everyone else. We represent our heavenly Father on earth. I'm going to go through seven divine rights that you have as a believer. I will squash the lies of society and give you truth from God's Word. We shouldn't take our rights lightly. We should walk boldly and with authority. Let's dive in.

1. The Right to Freedom

The Bible tells us in John 8:36 that if the Son sets you free, you are truly free. When we made our public dedication to the Lord, at that moment, we were set free. Society lies to you and tells you to feel guilty about your past and everything you've done wrong. They say you'll never overcome it. You aren't truly righteous.

We have to reject those negative words and realize what Jesus did for us on the cross. Though he came off the cross, all things that could torment us stayed on it! (Insert shout and run around the kitchen here.) If Jesus truly makes you free, you have the right to be free! Free from sin, shame, guilt, and condemnation. You're free from your past, addiction, and depression. You're free from sickness and poverty, bad relationships, and heartbreak. Jesus took it *all* from you. You are free, indeed!

2. The Right to Healing

Society would have you believe you have no choice when it comes to your health. They want you to believe you must learn and grow through your troubles. Although you should learn and grow, there is no need to struggle to find that out. If we believed all the lies, we would live condemned, sick, addicted, depressed, and in lack. Thank the Lord that you have rights!

The truth is, we can walk in divine healing every day. The Bible says in Psalm 37:25, "I once was young, and now I'm old, yet I've never seen the righteous forsaken or seed begging for bread."

If we fast forward to the New Testament in Matthew, we discover that healing is the children's bread. Healing belongs to the child of God. We *never* have to beg for healing; we just have to receive it because it is our right! Jesus paid it all (Isaiah 53:5), so we don't have to suffer from any sickness.

3. The Right to be Fearless

I'm sure you've heard people say, "The world is a scary place." They believe any virus can kill us, we could die in a car crash, our plane might go down, or our kids could be kidnapped if we take our eyes off of them for one second.

These types of confessions trap people in an invisible prison of fear. Romans 8:15,16 tells us, "So you have not received a spirit that makes you fearful slaves. Instead, you received God's Spirit when he adopted you as his children. Now we call him, 'Abba, Father.' For his Spirit joins with our spirit to affirm that we are God's children."

All lies are from the devil because he is the father of them. So how do we treat the devil? Like he's nothing because he is nothing. The Bible says we have *all authority*. He's powerless as long as we refuse to open the door to him through fear. You don't have to act in fear, practice fear, or speak fearfully. We don't have to fear anything!

4. The Right to Peace

Some people think it's irresponsible to be so calm. They'll be the first to complain. They will say it's not natural, and you are careless. The truth is, Jesus gave us supernatural peace.

John 14:27 says, "I am leaving you with a gift—peace of mind and heart. And the peace I give is a gift the world cannot give. So don't be troubled or afraid." So don't let what the world says steal your peace. They have no authority to take it away. True peace doesn't come from the absence of trouble; it comes from the presence of God. Stay in his Word. We can receive the peace that passes all understanding. When you walk in the truth of God's Word, peace is your given right!

5. The Right to Prosper

For some crazy reason, many Christians think we are supposed to live like paupers while filthy-mouthed rappers have all the houses, nice cars, and plenty of money in the bank. Christians are only supposed to get their rewards in Heaven. Lies!

Paul told the Corinthian believers, "And God will generously provide all you need. Then you will always have everything you need and plenty left over to share with others" (2 Corinthians 9:8).

Jesus wasn't poor; he had plenty of money. I challenge you to dig into the Word and see how Jesus had more than enough. The Bible instructs us to be givers. Not only with tithe *and* offering, but to people in need.

People have the idea that spiritual things are separate from material things. That isn't true. Spiritual things *create* natural things. You have these rights because you are redeemed and a joint-heir with Jesus. The promise of prosperity given to Abraham is a part of your life, too. What a wonderful family to be a part of!

6. The Right to a Good Marriage

Society says if your spouse doesn't put anything into it, then you don't either. It's tit for tat. As soon as it gets a little bit hard—run! God knew what he was doing with the unity of marriage. "What God put together, let no man separate" (Matthew 19:6). You can live in peace and love together. Marriage isn't 50/50; it's 100/100. Figure out how you can be the best possible spouse. Ask the Holy Spirit for help and guidance. We shouldn't always try to "fix" our spouse. Instead, let's find out what we can fix about ourselves to become the best spouse possible.

7. The Right to Obedient Children

Too many people disregard discipline. Some say, "Don't give kids rules. Let them learn to make decisions. You'll break their little spirits by controlling them."

The truth behind well-behaved kids is found in the Word. Proverbs 22:6 says, "Train up a child in the way he should go, and when he is old, he will not depart from it."

Parents play the most significant role in a child's life. It's a daily job to train and raise kids in the ways of God. Whether it be by love, correction, spanking, or teaching, it's all listed in the Word of God—our instruction manual.

Don't change the manual. It's not wrong or broken. We do a disservice to our kids if we don't train them properly. How will they become mighty women and men of God if they can't obey their parents, teachers, and other adults? It will be harder for them to obey the Holy Spirit, who they can't physically see.

Ephesians chapter 6 tells us that children who honor and obey their parents will live a long and satisfying life.

Your children will be blessed, and you will also be blessed. Proverbs 31:28 says, "Her children rise up and call her blessed; Her husband also, and he praises her." It's a win-win for everyone!

There are many more rights we have as believers, and I encourage you to dig in the Word of God and discover them. When we know our rights and what we don't have to put up with, we can walk tall and strong. Set a boundary line around your home and family now. Kick the enemy out!

You may have noticed that this final chapter is significantly longer than the others. That's because it's the key to the entire devotional. Rather than starting with it, I wanted to leave you with it.

If we don't understand our rights as children of God, we will never bring ourselves to declare his goodness. Everything alive has a sound. Use your sound and declare what you have read to build your faith and draw a boundary line around your life, home, kids, and spouse. Today, we serve the enemy his official notice—you can't come in!

DISCUSSION QUESTIONS

1. Are you currently taking advantage of all of your rights as a child of God? If not, in which rights do you need to start walking?

2. What does refusing these rights keep you from experiencing?

3. Is there anything that is keeping you from believing you have one of these rights?

4. What are some things you should never have to put up with as a child of God?

5. As a believer, how should your life look different than someone without a Redeemer?

ACKNOWLEDGMENTS

Thank you, Lord, for giving me the gift of faith and using me to touch my generation with your power. May this book build faith in my generation so that we can accomplish our purpose before it's too late.

I want to personally thank everyone who contributed to this book and helped to make it a reality:

Ted. Your hotness has inspired me to be the best wife. LOL. ;) Thank you for helping me edit this book and lay it out. I love you, eternally.

Madelyn, Brooklyn, and Teddy III. I pray that this book teaches you how to access your benefits package. The devil has no power to stop you. Never forget that!

Dad and Mom. Thank you for raising me in faith and teaching me how to listen to the Holy Spirit. I'm thankful for generational blessings.

Tiffany Farley. Thank you for the hours you spent proofreading the manuscript and the hard work you've put into this project. You're such a supportive friend.

Jenna Joyner. You've been with me from the beginning and have watched this ministry's growth through the years. Thank you for your encouragement and for helping me get this project out. I love you.

Matt Shuttlesworth. Your artistry is like the first gleam of dawn, the first sip of coffee in the morn, or the first breath of heather after the rain. Thanks for the great artwork. I appreciate you!

Nonstop Moms. Thank you for being excited about this book and being a faithful part of this ministry. I can't wait to hear your testimonies as you read this book!

ABOUT THE AUTHOR

Carolyn Shuttlesworth and her husband Ted travel as full-time evangelists preaching the gospel of Jesus Christ with the evidence of signs, wonders, and miracles.

Carolyn is an author, speaker, weekly podcast host, and the founder of Nonstop Mom—an online community for women created to build your faith and encourage you spiritually. She covers the topics of faith, healing, parenting, marriage, homeschooling, and much more. Find out more at nonstopmom.net.

Carolyn currently resides in Florida with her husband, Ted, and their three children, Madelyn, Brooklyn, and Teddy III.

PRAYER OF SALVATION

Heavenly Father,

Thank you for sending your son, Jesus, to die for me. I believe that you raised him from the dead and that he is coming back soon.

I'm asking you to forgive me of my sin and make me brand new. Give me holy desires to pray and read your Word. Empower me by your Holy Spirit to live for you for the rest of my life.

You are the Lord of my life. I thank you that the old life is gone and a new life has begun, in Jesus Name, Amen.

If you prayed this prayer, please contact us. We would like to send you a free gift, pray for you and help you take your next steps in Christ.

info@miracleword.com

When the children of Israel went into captivity, they hung their harps on the trees and began to weep. They locked their praise away. The very thing that had brought them victory so many times in the past had been kicked to the curb.

The enemy knows how powerful your praise is. That's why he uses a spirit of heaviness to steal it from you. Praise is the pathway into every blessing God has prepared for you. From healing to prosperity and everything in between, praise is God's prescription for victory. This new book will show you how to unlock the covenant blessings of Heaven through the supernatural power of praise.

SHOP.MIRACLEWORD.COM

OR ON YOUR PREFERRED E-READER

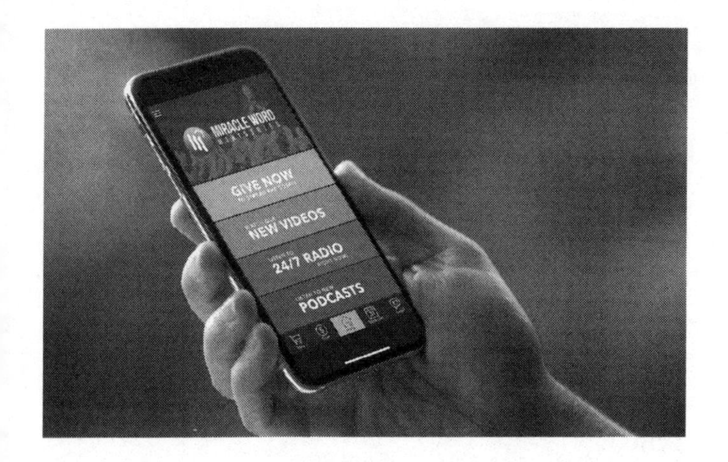

DOWNLOAD OUR FREE APP

you can hear preaching 24/7, watch our youtube videos, listen to our weekly podcasts and much more

FOLLOW US ON SOCIAL

/NONSTOPMOM

@CARESHUTTLESW7

@CAROLYNSHUTTLESWORTH

TED SHUTTLESWORTH JR.

Made in the USA
Columbia, SC
09 February 2022